SOMEBODY'S GOTTA DO IT

SOMEBODY'S GOTTA DO IT

Why Cursing at the News
Won't Save the Nation, but Your
Name on a Local Ballot Can

ADRIENNE MARTINI

HENRY HOLT AND COMPANY

NEW YORK

Henry Holt and Company
Publishers since 1866
120 Broadway
New York, New York 10271
www.henryholt.com

Henry Holt® and ® are registered trademarks of
Macmillan Publishing Group, LLC.

Library of Congress Cataloging-in-Publication Data is available

ISBN: 9781250247636

Epigraph text reprinted with permission from
Daniel Alexander Jones, *Black Light*, 2015

Our books may be purchased in bulk for promotional, educational,
or business use. Please contact your local bookseller or the Macmillan
Corporate and Premium Sales Department at (800) 221-7945, extension
5442, or by email at MacmillanSpecialMarkets@macmillan.com.

First Edition 2020

Designed by Meryl Sussman Levavi

Map by Lisa Horstman

Printed in the United States of America

1   3   5   7   9   10   8   6   4   2

What if I told you it's going to be alright?

What if I told you not yet?

What if I told you there are trials ahead beyond your deepest fears?

What if I told you you will fall down, down, down?

What if I told you you will surprise yourself?

What if I told you you will be brave . . . enough?

—*Black Light*, Daniel Alexander Jones

Contents

Introduction

You are angry. You are afraid. Given all that has happened in recent years, you can't see how to get this country back on a sane path, one with protections for the most vulnerable people and our environment. And one where every person—no matter their race, economic status, or sexual orientation—is treated equally under the law.

In 2019, the nation's prospects were made even more harrowing by the Supreme Court decision that, according to a very narrow interpretation of centuries of case law, gerrymandering is A-OK. The consequences of this could be grim. As Justice Elena Kagan wrote in her dissent: "These gerrymanders enabled politicians to entrench themselves in office as against voters' preferences."

The way forward feels impossible to see. I hear you. I am you.

Even though the power of positive thinking is part of why we're here, it is true that every crisis also contains opportunity. Dig deep and discover your joyful warrior within. The only way out of this is to convert all that fear and ire and disgust into action. Small steps matter, especially if we hold hands and take them together.

Right now, there is a ripe, juicy opportunity ready to be plucked. The redistricting that will happen in 2021 will set electoral maps for a decade. Now is the time to run for local or state office (or support someone who is) because those offices have the most influence on how districts are drawn. When IS now exactly? It's . . . well, it's now. You might want to read this book first, but then, after that, immediately after that—is now.

"Whether you are a Republican or a Democrat watching right now, if you know someone who ought to run for something, or if you ought to run for something, the thing you ought to run for is the state legislature in your state," Rachel Maddow said. "And you better do it right now."

This book offers some hints and tips about running for local office but isn't a how-to. Other books, such as Amanda Litman's *Run for Something: A Real-Talk Guide to Fixing the System Yourself*, will give you an action plan for getting in the game. The book you have in your hands (or on your screen) is, instead, your companion while you do what Amanda tells you to do. *Somebody's Gotta Do It* is an experienced (okay, slightly experienced) friend to anyone who wants to rebuild and reimagine what America can be. The officeholders at the top of the system can only do so much without working with the elected representatives at the bottom. This book will show you that you (yes, you!) are somebody who can make a difference. And this book will keep you company when it feels like too much. It isn't too much, really. Sort of. And anyway, even when on occasion it is a *lot*, somebody's gotta do it.

SOMEBODY'S GOTTA DO IT

CHAPTER 1

Leap, Then Look

If you are truly following the tenets of Oprah and living your best life, you will have at least one moment in your existence when you realize that the water you landed in after your leap of faith is miles over your head. You are down in the Mariana Trench with the luminous fish who have become so adapted to the pressures of the briny deep that they will explode if brought to the surface. You are that far out of your depth.

I've had three of those moments. The first was when I moved from my native Pittsburgh to Austin, Texas, to follow some guy when he moved there for grad school. The second was when I had my first child. And the third took place in a lovely, if generic, meeting room in December 2017.

There was a giant Christmas tree in one corner and maybe seventy-five seats in front of a podium. We had breakfast nibbles and coffee to fuss with while we listened to a presentation on the different forms of county government and which would work best for Otsego County. I was one of the incoming representatives on the county board, soon to be sworn in on a bitterly cold New Year's Day.

Our county is the only one in New York that uses the Board

of Representatives model—that is, fourteen representatives, one for each district, but no county executive; thus, every single decision is made by the fourteen-member committee. Many of the incoming reps had run on changing that Board of Reps system because it is wildly inefficient and keeps us from being able to focus on issues bigger than budget modifications and mandated training.

◎ ◎ ◎

After that forms-of-government Q&A session ended—during which there was the usual mix of good questions and remarks by dudes with more of a comment than a question—the reps-elect were pulled aside for a quick overview with the county treasurer on how the budget works. In less than an hour, the treasurer planned to download the entirety of a $105 million operation into our heads, complete with spreadsheets full of itty-bitty numbers. (Not that the amounts were itty-bitty: The highway department's salt-and-sand line item alone could have paid for my house three times over, which was sobering. No, I mean the numerals themselves: they were in tiny 2-point type so the treasurer could print them all out without using up several reams of paper.)

The treasurer explained that the county's income derives from property taxes coupled with "beds, meds, and eds," the income from tourism, our two big hospitals, and the two colleges. Then there was the income we generated from acting as a giant funnel for all sorts of dollars from state and federal agencies.

That's good, I thought. I understand how the money comes in.

Then he told us how the money goes out. The short list of what the county does includes social services such as foster care, mental health services including treatments for substance dependency, road maintenance, a jail and law enforcement, emergency services, solid waste disposal, code enforcement, vaccines, public transportation, legal services, coroners, and tourism marketing. Oh, and we'd like to keep our green spaces green and our watersheds blue. We'd also like not to have our elderly and infirm residents starve or freeze.

Two pages into the spreadsheets, I had a moment like the one I had when I was a fresh college grad calling home from a grimy street pay phone in Austin to let my family know that my boyfriend and I had successfully navigated our way south and unpacked what little we had. I'd obsessed over how to get everything there, but now I needed to find a job in August in a weird city with its external thermostat stuck on broil.

This budget overview session also recalled that moment when I first held my own baby and realized that I'd spent the previous nine months obsessed with the wrong things. I owned every book on pregnancy and delivery, but had no skills or knowledge about, you know, infants.

I'd approached running for office armed with research and numbers and opinions about how to win, rather than collecting information about what happens once you're sworn in. I'd won, damn it, against an incumbent who was relatively well liked. It felt like a minor miracle for a woman who hadn't been politically engaged until November 2016.

When you're at that pay phone in a new city, wondering where to start; when the baby finally arrives and cries and cries and cries; when you read the budget with the minuscule type— that's when you have your David Byrne moment: "My God! What have I done?"

◦ ◦ ◦

I spent the Monday before Election Day 2016 on a train speeding up the Hudson River's eastern shore. Even though I am not a native New York Stater, I'd made this trip from the big, bad city back to my rural upstate home often enough to know that the seats on the left side of the car are the best because your view out over the water is unobscured. After fifteen-plus years here, I know a few of the river's moods, from summer's calm blue to late winter's turbulent brown. On this November Monday, sunshine poured through the leafless trees and the water looked as if it had been sprinkled with glitter.

This may have been a hallucination.

The Sunday before that Monday in November, I did something so exhausting and amazing that my brain was a wrung-out sponge, despite a decent night's sleep in a decadent mid-priced hotel bed. As the train rocked (and with a steady dose of ibuprofen in my system), my body felt as if it had been beaten with a pillowcase full of oranges. Yet, I was in a state of bliss, coasting on endorphins. I had a big shiny medal hanging around my neck. A dude sitting kitty-corner from me had a medal on, too.

On that Sunday before the Monday, that random dude, fifty thousand other people, and I had run the New York City Marathon, not at all a thing I thought I'd be doing even a year before I did it. And five years before that, even the idea of a 5K, which is twenty-three fewer miles than a marathon, was daunting. It's taken me a couple of decades to recognize my habit of escalating any given leisure activity to a stupid, epic goal. I didn't start running until I turned forty. Six years later, I committed to a marathon. Once I have a good idea, I can't resist seeing just how far I can push it.

On the train that Monday, I was still riding the high of having run 26.2 miles, from Staten Island to the Isle of Manhattan. My legs had failed to fall off; nor had I crumpled into a heap,

sobbing, on a First Avenue curb. I didn't decide to jump on
the subway at mile 13, even though I had a MetroCard in the
pocket of my running skirt. Whenever I was tired or bored or
sore, I switched my playlist over to the *Hamilton* soundtrack.
How many people can run down the streets of the greatest city
in the world? Even as we were in the middle of doing incredibly hard things, like running for hours and hours for no good
reason, all of us were so lucky to be alive right then. Not only
were we having an epic Sunday morning, but in forty-eight
hours, our great experiment of a country would elect its first
female president.

Running long distances always brings out my thinkiest
thoughts. And, yes, anyone who runs a marathon will, when
given the slightest opening, blather on about running a marathon. We know it's annoying. We don't care.

In the same amount of time it takes four generations of
fruit flies to be born, mate, need bifocals, and die, I crossed the
finish line. Seconds after being handed my medal and a bagful
of snacks, I called my husband, who was at home with our son,
and sobbed happy, amazed tears at him. After a slow shuffle to
Columbus Circle, right across from the Trump International
Hotel and Tower, I hooked up with the posse of friends who'd
chased me across the city with my teenage daughter. There
were many more happy tears, and mind-blowing disbelief.
Everyone laughed with me as I winced my way down the subway steps; everyone helped me back to my hotel, where I took
a shower, ate all the food in the room, and went to sleep.

Before the marathon, I had been sensible enough to take a
couple of days off from my job writing and editing the alumni
magazine for SUNY Oneonta. We'd moved to Oneonta fourteen years earlier because my husband had been offered a job
in the theatre department. Once we figured out where it was
(between Binghamton and Albany on the I-88), we hit the road

with three cats and one fourteen-month-old. We'd been ready to get the heck out of Tennessee (long story) and closer to our families, which were scattered around the Northeast. Oneonta seemed as good a place as any. Plus, the college had a teaching gig for me, one that I could easily juggle with a toddler daughter.

That toddler is now a teenager, and has a younger brother, and we've never found a reason to leave. Oneonta suits us. When my dad retired, he moved here from Columbus, Ohio, because he wanted to be able to see his grandchildren more frequently and because there wasn't much keeping him in Ohio. He'd moved to the Buckeye State decades before for a job, not for family.

One of the features I most enjoy about Oneonta is how close it is to New York City while still being so far away. If the traffic cooperates, I can drive to any number of train stations and be in Midtown Manhattan in under four hours. But we're just enough off the beaten path—there is no direct train service from New York City to here—that we don't get weekenders driving up our house prices and grousing about our lack of Uber Eats.

After my Monday morning post-marathon breakfast of eggs and a waffle at a diner, I was home by the afternoon. I started a load of extra-stinky laundry and was unconscious in my own bed by 7 p.m. What I wanted to do on Tuesday, Election Day, was swan around in my jammies. Still, I put on my grown-up pants long enough to gimp down to our local polling place because I was excited to put an end to this bitter election season.

I knew my county would go for Trump because I live in a very red part of a very blue state. I felt a little thrill when I filled in the bubble next to Hillary Clinton's name on my ballot. I even, briefly, wished that my kids were still young enough to force to the polling place with me. A few of my fondest memories are of the old mechanical voting machines and lugging whichever preschooler was the most cooperative that day into the booth so that he or she could pull the big lever that recorded my vote. They, naturally, were in it for the "I Voted" sticker, which the senior citizens who worked at the polls would happily give them.

By November 2016, my kids were far too busy to come watch me fill in a paper ballot with a Sharpie and then feed the ballot into an optical scanner. I still miss the hearty *ka-chunk* of the old machines. That noise really leant some gravitas to exercising one's hard-won franchise.

After casting my vote for HRC, I spent the rest of the day napping or scrolling through social media. I caught a video on Facebook from the National Women's Hall of Fame, which is only a few hours from my house. Women were putting their "I Voted" stickers on Susan B. Anthony's headstone. Now, that would be a fun field trip, I thought, once I feel like moving around again.

After the polls closed, some friends and family members announced on social media that they were proud #deplorables and just could not vote for "that woman." I didn't give it much thought at the time, other than to wonder why they'd waited so long to come out as supporters of Donald Trump. If you were so proud of your nominee, why didn't you shout it from the electronic rooftops months ago?

No matter. Confronting my mom and aunts and in-laws and cousins and internet friends wasn't something I needed to do, because there was no way their Trumpian mind-set was in the majority. Given how weary I was, I nearly went to bed before the polls in New York State closed at 9 p.m. Staying up to see Hillary declared our next president seemed beyond my capabilities.

It's almost funny now how confident so many of us were. If this had been a movie—if only the past few years were fictional—the audience would have been shouting at the screen, begging the main characters to open their damn eyes.

Each one of us, Democrat and Republican alike, has his or her own take on the shock of that night. Trump voters responded with glee at the unexpected turn of the electorate. This Democrat spent the bulk of the night curled up in bed texting my husband, who was at work. I couldn't stop shaking. I eventually popped a Tylenol PM and fell into a drug-induced sleep.

In the morning, my husband and I had to tell the kids how wrong we'd been about Trump's popularity and that even some people we knew well had voted for him. Yes, it was baffling. Yes, we'd spent the last three months assuring them that there was no way Trump would win. And, yes, sometimes your parents are flat-out wrong.

CHAPTER 2

Not Ready to Make Nice

Most people who didn't vote for Trump, which would be most voters, spent the weeks from Election Day to his inauguration in various stages of the Kubler-Ross model of grief. Personally, I moved through denial pretty quickly. I did get a little hung up on bargaining. My hope was that someone might undo what had been done, despite my knowing the Constitution well enough to understand that there is no Ctrl+Z subclause. I gave twenty dollars to Jill Stein's alleged recount and, yes, I was ashamed in hindsight. I thought the "Hamilton Electors" gambit had a chance, but not one greater than a snowball's survival in Arizona in August. (In case you've forgotten, because it seems like a billion years since November 2016, the Hamilton Electors/Faithless Electors movement attempted to get members of the Electoral College to change their vote when it came time to formalize the results of the election. For your next game of Trivial Pursuit: The only time that more than a few electors have done this was in 1872, when their preferred candidate died. But even then, their defections from the dead guy didn't change the result of the election itself and only added more electoral votes to Grant's already apparent victory.)

Bargaining, however, was the act of a woman grasping at any piece of debris that might keep her afloat for a few more minutes. A deep, dark quicksand of anger was oozing around my ankles. After Thanksgiving, to which one of my husband's uncles wore his MAGA hat, I let the quicksand take me. True, I woke up every morning promising that today would be different. Today, I would make peace with the Trump supporters around me and do my best to understand their economic anxiety. But any such vow would be undone seconds after I checked the previous night's news. By evening, prodded by the events of the day, I'd go to bed on the verge of biting someone. Every "What Trump Voters Feel" piece made my jaw clench. Every "Both Candidates Had Flaws" conversation left me wanting to punch someone. I wanted to scream "He's going to eat you first" to every single Trump voter I met.

Melodramatic? Sure. But you had your own wailing-and-rending-your-garments moment, didn't you, even if you didn't literally wail or rend? It was a fraught few months as we came to terms with what had happened and started to wrap our minds around what was coming.

In hindsight, we had no idea how truly weird it was going to get.

Before the 2016 presidential election, I wasn't anything close to a political animal. While I passed the basic civics course everyone had to take in high school in the late 1980s, back in the halcyon days when the Soviet Union was likely to nuke us, I hadn't interacted with government systems at more than a rudimentary level since then. In college, I spent my social science credits on history classes. The first time I voted was for Hillary Clinton's husband's second term, and I've had an unbroken streak of voting for presidents since then. Most of the candidates I'd voted for failed to win.

Once my husband and I settled in Upstate New York, I also

voted for local stuff, like the school board or county sheriff, when those offices were being contested. But that wasn't often, because most local races had only one candidate, generally a Republican incumbent. For years, the local Democratic Party didn't make a strong play for these small offices. After 2016, everyone saw this was a terrible strategy because these offices, first, aren't expensive to contest, and second, have way more impact on a person's daily life than state or federal politics does. We can argue until there is no more oxygen left on the planet about trickle-down tax plans or universal health care, but those issues don't matter if everyone in your neighborhood has rabies because the county Board of Health has no money.

Back in the fall of 2016, I knew nothing about the Board of Health. I did know who my senators were, though I wasn't too sure who my representative in the U.S. House was. I had a vague inkling who my state reps were, if only because they would send flyers every fall to remind me of their existence. I was solid on knowing who my city and county guys were (and they were all guys). They'd actually come to my house personally to woo me, a perk of being a reliable voter in a small town in a sparsely populated region.

Like most nonpolitical animals, I considered politicians sort of oily. My thinking has been that anyone who wants that job shouldn't have it. Anyone who runs for office has to have made questionable compromises to get there. Since we're given the option to vote only for human beings, which means there is no such thing as ethical perfection in a candidate, it's just a matter of choosing the one who is the least tainted.

Before the election season of 2016, I would have described myself as ambivalently progressive. While my country is imperfect—see my previous comment about being able to vote only for human beings, all of whom are imperfect—I believed we were largely on a path toward all men and women being equal in the eyes of the law. I took for granted that despite setbacks and false starts, the long arc of history was bending toward justice without my personally needing to go to protests or write my legislators or do anything more than show up at the voting booth and pull the lever.

I understand now that political ambivalence is easy when you are a middle-class, middle-aged white woman with a decent education. While our system is rigged for white men, straight white women have had a lot break our way, too. Few of the men in power want to pursue legislation that will cause us active harm (mostly because we remind most legislators of their moms and wives), and few of the men in power need to actively court us because we've been pretty laissez-faire about advocating for our interests.

Sure, I'd been on board with the idea of a higher minimum wage to help single moms stay out of poverty. Increased parental leave and stronger workforce protections for an equal wage regardless of gender would also be swell. And I believed that women's health care and family planning services should be accessible even if you're living in poverty. But none of these issues affected me personally at this point in my life. I'm done with having babies, and those babies are now big enough to not want me with them every moment of the day. My workplace is largely unionized, which means we enjoy a whole raft of protections denied to others. Like any parent, I worried about the world my daughter would walk into, but I knew she'd have the means to be okay, if only because she lives in a state that supports women controlling their own bodies.

A few years after we moved here, my husband and I and our then-early-elementary-school-aged kids were having dinner with another family. The husband, Karl, is an economics professor at the private college in town. His wife, Kate, is a labor delivery lactation RN. Our kids are the same ages and, because this is a small city, went to the same schools. While the four younglings were upstairs making Kate and Karl's playroom look like it had been through a Jim Cantore–level weather event, the adults did what adults do, which is talk about things other than video games marketed to eight-year-olds.

I can't remember what Republican outrage Karl and I were talking about, mostly because it was at the end of the George W. Bush era and there were just so many outrages to choose from. But at some point, Karl mentioned that it was only a matter of time before a revolution broke out. Not yet, I said. We're too comfortable.

This was before the Black Lives Matter movement helped me realize how complicit I was in where the country was on race. I wasn't "woke," and #MeToo wasn't yet a thing. Was I angry about systemic inequality? Not really. I knew that the average, mediocre middle-aged white guy would always suc-ceed faster than anyone else, same as it ever was. White men always fail upward. Just look at who the president was.

But regardless of who the president was, I was resigned to watching from the sidelines, where I'd built a comfortable bench, complete with Orla Kiely cushions and a Starbucks skinny white chocolate mocha. Like so many in my circle, I had the privilege to snark that I would move to Canada if polit-ical winds shifted in a direction that caused me personal harm. But now, years later, after Trump's victory, somewhere during my weeks of anger, I had a very small epiphany: If Trump and his supporters wanted to strip away decades of progress, there was no way I was leaving. They'd have to get through me and, as it was slowly becoming clear, thousands of women like me. Our years of comfort had made it look like we were getting closer to equality, only for us to learn that our freedoms hadn't really been won so much as temporarily granted for the sake of keeping us complacent—to say nothing of the freedoms and rights of people who didn't look like us.

The 2016 election stomped all over the pleasant illusions I'd embroidered during the Obama years. In fact, the destruction of my illusions might be what pissed me off the most.

CHAPTER 3

American Carnage Meets Pink Pussyhats

On a normal workday, the idea of spending six hours in a quasi-annual divisional retreat sounds about as fun as having your gums scraped. While I love talking with my clever coworkers about how to build connections between our alumni and the college, sitting in one room staring at PowerPoint slides and doing SWOT analyses (Strengths, Weaknesses, Opportunities, and Threats) ordinarily makes me want to weep.

But on Inauguration Day 2017, I fell into the SWOT work retreat as if it were a down duvet on a subzero day. For six hours, I would know nothing about what was going on in the world outside the conference room's doors. I would save Trump's swearing in for the evening, when I could digest it in manageable bits in my own house and snark about it with my husband. Unfortunately, I forgot there was a TV just outside the conference room.

During our lunch break, a couple of us stood in front of it, unable to turn away. The cameras panned over what looked like a sparse crowd wearing red baseball caps as Trump launched into his address.

"Mothers and children trapped in poverty in our inner

cities, rusted-out factories, scattered like tombstones across the landscape of our nation, an education system flush with cash but which leaves our young and beautiful students deprived of all knowledge and the crime and the gangs and the drugs that have stolen too many lives and robbed our country of so much unrealized potential. This American carnage stops right here and stops right now."

I honestly have no idea what we did in our afternoon SWOT session. Maybe we talked about return on investment? Alumni engagement? Perhaps we made plans for invading other SUNY campuses, given that we now lived in a carnage-filled *Mad Max* hellscape. It is a mystery that will be lost to time. Somehow, despite the gangs and the drugs and the tombstones, we all survived the night. I'm shocked, too.

But the morning after the inauguration, I saw on my living room television a marvelous wonder that helped dispel the myth of a country entirely in steep decline: a sea of handmade pink pussyhats on the National Mall in DC, Boston, and New York City. As a knitter (another leisure activity I'd at one time pushed to a stupid epic goal), I'd produced a few of those hats myself as a way to channel some of my anger into a marginally productive activity. Among knitters, pussyhats became like that Amish friendship bread recipe passed from baker to baker since time began.

Los Angeles–based Jayna Zweiman and Krista Suh cofounded the Pussyhat Project when Krista planned to go to the Women's March in DC and Jayna couldn't join her. Kat Coyle, owner of the Little Knittery yarn shop, also in LA, designed a dead-easy knitting pattern, a shade of pink yarn was grabbed, and history was made. I can't even remember how I heard about the pussyhats, only that suddenly every knitter I knew was making one. A yarn dyer friend, Jennifer Tepper, worked up a range of pinks named after prominent women and donated a portion of the proceeds of their sale to women's nonprofits. My favorite color was a deep pink named after Jarena Lee, one of the first African American women authorized to preach in the African Methodist Episcopal Church in the early 1800s.

For most of November and December, I carried hats in progress wherever I went. A modern-day Madame Defarge, I knitted on my sofa while watching the news, only with decidedly less beheading. Those months felt weightless, as if I were watching the ground rush up to meet me but wasn't quite sure if the impact would be fatal or merely debilitating. The knitting occupied my hands enough to keep the panic at bay.

Because this is a polarized time, controversy erupted over the hats. A yarn shop owner near Nashville deemed both the march and the hats "vulgar and vile." Trump's now-imprisoned personal attorney Michael Cohen insinuated that the hats had been mass-produced in China, simply because he couldn't wrap his head around the notion of individual women having made so many of them. And, of course, the "pussy" set some teeth on edge, even though it is a body part our president has bragged about grabbing.

Video from the news networks tracked marches across the globe, each characterized by their seas of pink. Here are pink hats gathered in front of the Eiffel Tower. Here they are on the streets of Philadelphia, London, San Francisco, and Nairobi. Women, some in pink hats, some with clever signs, took over the world's public spaces that day, and we all felt slightly less alone.

As you look closer at the images, you will see how different each of the hats in the sea is. Every shade of pink turns up, as does all manner of handicraft. The ones that struck me most were the simplest: a rectangle of pink polar fleece fabric folded in half and sewn up the sides. I admired them all, however, no matter if they were knitted, crocheted, or sewn.

Each woman who made a hat, whether for herself or for the common cause, approached the project in her own way, with her own set of skills. You don't need me to connect all of the dots in this metaphor. On a personal level, what might have been most important, beyond the big public statements these marchers made, was how seeing that many women as angry as I was made me feel less alone.

A few of the pink hats I'd knitted were on the heads of friends who traveled the six hours to DC. Two of the hats stayed local for Oneonta's own march. A couple of hundred people (a Woodstock-size crowd for here) turned out in our most public space, the town square, which, depending on the season, is home to the farmers' market, Santa's house, or a giant menorah. Of course, the local Bernie Bros and MAGA Men made an appearance at the march, but they were vastly outnumbered by the pink.

Just to add a little poignancy, said town square is named after Kim Muller, the city's first female mayor, who was sworn in by Otsego County's first female judge in 1997. Muller, who retired from office in 2005, lives just around the corner from me and still tears it up in local politics on the regular—but as a Democratic Party member, rather than a candidate herself. There were rumors that once HRC had sewn up the presidency, Muller would be tapped for a regional position by Hillary and wind up running the state-level branch of a federal agency devoted to eliminating poverty or increasing access to education. Now we'll never know what federally sanctioned good she might have done.

The local pussyhats bobbing around Muller Plaza leant an emotional echo to Muller's groundbreaking mayoral run, and the pussyhats across the globe were a great piece of visual marketing. The images that came out of those marches will always be united by their expanses of pink, a color that will forever mark this particular moment in history, and make it so that Trump's media team can't pass off these immense crowds as his—inspired by him, yes, just not in a way he'd like.

Those photos showed a revolution beginning. In a few decades, I hope that the musical *Pussyhat*, penned by Lin-Manuel Miranda's kids, maybe, wins all the Tonys. For future historians who will read this and ask if the mid-2010s were really as relentlessly nuts as they seemed: you can't even imagine. And for those future historians, here's one way we managed to survive the flood of crazy: the pink pussyhats reminded us that we can make things, including metaphoric boats that keep us above the waterline.

◌ ◌ ◌

In a 2018 essay for *The Nation* that commemorated the one-year anniversary of the Women's March, Katha Pollitt wrote about the women who, like me, realized they weren't going to go to Canada after all, but were going to stay and fight for justice. And one true hope of mine is that the title of Pollitt's essay winds up being the subtitle of the entire Trump era: "We Are Living Through the Moment When Women Unleash Decades of Pent-up Anger."

In her essay, Pollitt notes that after the 2016 election, "[According] to the app Daily Action, 86 percent of active callers to Congress were women—particularly middle-aged women, the most overlooked people in Punditland. Good old Mom, so boring, so ordinary, so unphotogenic!"

Like Pollitt, I'm waiting for the breathless think piece about how these women feel. As she writes, "I suppose that won't happen as long as there are small-town diners full of angry white men in MAGA hats."

As petty as it seems, the media focus on the men in MAGA hats rather than on the millions of women across the globe who marched is what got under my skin, because it proved what we've known to be true but what many of us never fully acknowledged: the opinion of a single mediocre white man is considered more valuable than those of an enormous sea of women.

I thought we'd come a long way, baby, to echo the Virginia Slims ads of a million years ago. Even with all the tiny moments of sexism every single woman endures in her lifetime, I had felt that we were making some significant progress and that my daughter's generation would inherit a smarter world.

For me, the realization that this wasn't the case resembled that scene in the Christmas movie *Elf* where Will Ferrell's character, Buddy, a normal guy who was raised in the North Pole by toy-making elves, confronts a department store Santa. This particular Santa isn't at all like the Santa whom Buddy grew up around. The interaction ends with Buddy yelling, with all the betrayal his voice can hold, at this random guy in a Santa suit, "You sit on a throne of lies." In America, the idea of an equal playing field is a throne of lies. And, yes, I know that people of color and gender-nonconforming people and Muslims and many others knew this already. Call me slow on the uptake, and I'm sorry about that. Truly, I am. But I've got the memo now.

Anyway, as cathartic as the march was, once it was over, there was nowhere for all this rage to go. My usual outlet for any upheaval is to toss on my running shoes and pound some pavement until my inner voice shuts the heck up for a bit. But since I'd run my marathon, which I will continue to tell you about, I wasn't running as much or as often as needed to burn off some of my excess emotion. Add to that, one of my hips wasn't keen on the fact that it had carried me for twenty-six miles, and it wasn't in any mood to do it for another mile, much less around the block. With all that, my usual method of dealing with strong emotions was gone.

I compensated by being alternately surly to everyone around me or unable to leave my bed, where I just wanted to hide, eat all the carbs in the house, and read books I already knew by heart. These are not good ways to cope with long-term problems. Eventually, I would be like a bottle of soda that had been shaken. When the cap came off, we were going to need a mop and a new kitchen.

When I had the energy, I did what I could to bleed off some of the rage. I knitted an ocean of pussyhats, which were still being worn to organizing events after the march. I wrote post-cards and called my representatives, as I'd been told to do by the organizations that grew out of the Women's March. Phone calling took the edge off, but seemed sort of futile, especially when the response was either a form letter—Rep. John Faso really appreciated my concerns about the degradation of democracy but would like me to just calm down (I'm paraphrasing)—or sass from whichever of Faso's college-age interns was forced to answer phones that day. That's when I got any response at all. Most of the time there was silence or a busy signal—but mostly silence.

Silence, by the way, only made the rage worse, because it confirmed just how little my opinion mattered to those in power, which I had known subconsciously but never before acknowledged. Couple that with the cascade of executive orders Trump signed during his first few weeks in office. From an attempt to dismantle the Affordable Care Act to his Muslim ban, they made it pretty clear pretty quickly that the GOP in power was going to do exactly what they said they were going to do, which was put the screws to anyone not straight, white, male, and Christian. I knew then I had to do more than write a few postcards and stew.

CHAPTER 4

A New York State of Mind

We need to talk about New York for a second.

When I say New York, most of the images that pop into non–New Yorkers' brains are of Times Square, the Statue of Liberty, and the Chrysler Building. You imagine enormous masses of rude people rushing around and dodging yellow cabs. If you think of green spaces, you think of Central Park.

But that is *not* New York State. (And it's really not even New York City, but that's beyond the scope of this information dump.)

New York State is the fourth-most-populous state in the nation. There are roughly 19 million New York State residents, and it is a reliably blue state when it comes to national elections.

The itty-bitty little island is Manhattan, where 1.67 million people (give or take) live. If you count the population of that island plus that of the four other boroughs (Staten Island, Brooklyn, Queens, and the Bronx) that surround it, and that together make up the City of New York, you get 8.62 million people. One of my favorite sayings about the sheer number of bodies in that space was on a billboard years ago: "One in a Million?" it asked. "There are eight of you here." Now, if

you add in 4.9 million people living in the counties within a ninety-minute drive of Manhattan, you'll find two-thirds of the state's population lives in one megalopolis. Those big-city-plus-its-suburbs people are the reason the state goes blue.

The other 6.4 million people fill the rest of the surface area in this large state. Most of them live closer to Cleveland or Boston or Burlington than to New York City. Most live within thirty minutes of big cities such as Albany, Syracuse, Rochester, and Buffalo. One of the less populated parts of the state is called the North Country and is where most of the Adirondack Park is. Drive just a few minutes north from most of the North Country, and you're in Canada.

In the middle of the state, there are the Finger Lakes, a region known for wine, cheese, and the Ivy League university Cornell. Scoot just a little east from the Finger Lakes and a little west of the Catskills, and you hit Otsego County.

If you could find a way to evenly scatter the people who live here, you'd have sixty-two people per square mile. But Otsego

Countians aren't evenly scattered, which is a pity, because that would be incredibly convenient. Most live in Oneonta, which has a population equivalent to a quarter of a New York City square mile, or Cooperstown, which has the same number of people as live in a smallish New York City apartment building. You are well aware of Cooperstown if you're any sort of baseball fan. Yes, the Hall of Fame is lovely. And, yes, locals both love and hate Hall of Fame induction weekend because we love tourists' dollars but bemoan the increased traffic.

Those two hubs are surrounded and separated by acres and acres of farmland, forest, rivers, mountains, and lakes. It is beautiful country in the spring, summer, and fall. Its winter beauty is harder to appreciate, but you grow to love it in a Stockholm syndrome kind of way.

Otsego County, like the majority of New York's rural counties, is politically deep, deep red. If we only counted the votes from the rural parts of New York State, Trump would have won the popular vote in New York by a landslide. But because the population around New York City is so liberal and so populous, you'll never see all of New York State in red on a national election map.

On a state government level, this divide causes no end of arguing. Downstaters are tired of all their tax money flowing upstate, which downstaters define as anything outside New York City. Upstaters are ticked off that the crumbling New York City subway system gets far more attention than the urgent need for rural job opportunities. Every few years, the debate about upstate seceding from downstate is reignited, and all parties eventually agree on one thing: that all the state's sixty-two counties are better together. Another point that all parties agree on is that the governor doesn't understand any issue he takes on, which is a puzzle, given that he is popular enough to keep getting reelected.

Those are the two points of unity in a state full of political divides. Just like every single state in the union, New York isn't as united as you'd hope. Somehow, though, we continue to muddle through.

In the run-up to the 2016 presidential election, I'd scoped out the OCDC, the Otsego County Democratic Committee. I figured I could make a phone call or two for Hillary, even though I knew she didn't stand a chance of carrying my county, which had preferred Bernie in the Democratic primary. But the OCDC's website didn't fill me with hope, or initiative— mostly because there wasn't much there. The website seemed more focused on social events than political action. I didn't even bother getting in contact with them.

After the birth of my rage in early 2017, though, I reached out to Dave, a friend of a friend. Years ago, I'd coached his daughter in Girls on the Run, a national nonprofit whose mission is to develop confidence in elementary-age girls by training them to run a 5K. I'd also nearly lost this daughter of his in the elementary school we were using as our base when I miscounted how many kids I had at the end of one of the practices. (She was fine, by the way, having wandered off to the library to read rather than run.) Hopefully, Dave would be willing to let bygones be bygones.

When I first contacted him, my initial thought was to help the OCDC with phone calls or fundraising or whatever it is that local branches of national parties do when the country is on fire. Maybe, I thought, it would feel as if I were actually doing something to "hashtag resist" if I were part of a traditional structure and not just writing postcards in my dining room.

Dave suggested setting up a time to talk at his house, which is just around the corner from mine. He made it sound like a formal meeting rather than just a quick "here's who you need to call and, hey, give us some money" chitchat. Because Dave has always struck me as a pretty formal guy in general—for example, I don't know that I've ever seen him in a T-shirt—I didn't think too much about his serious tone. At his house, though, the penny dropped when he said, "Would you consider running for the county board?"

What Dave couldn't hear (I think) was the hysterical laughter inside my head. I'm a middle-aged mom of two who makes her living shoving words around. I have a degree in theater, for Pete's sake, and have written two books, including, most recently, one about knitting, a subject that important people who make policy don't give two craps about. I am not a politician. Politicians understand how to manipulate public opinion, boss around the tax code, and make sure the sewers work. I can't even manipulate those to whom I gave birth, and I had once nearly lost Dave's eight-year-old in an empty school building.

While I sat there blinking, he made his case: The county board has two-year terms and its members are up for election every odd year. The incumbent representative for our district, a Republican, would likely run unopposed in November 2017. During his past four years on the board, he had made some regressive choices, frequently hadn't shown up, and when he was there, it could be argued, he generally stood in the way of progress. He's beatable, Dave said, if someone smart, personable, and game was willing to give it a try.

I told him I'd think about it, which was a lie. Why would I do something that was silly from its very beginning? I am not a strong candidate. To pick just one small example, in high school, I lit my bangs on fire lighting a cigarette on a gas stove. In my defense, it was the '80s, and the bangs were very big and held in place by gallons of Aqua Net. Still, I can't picture Elizabeth Warren ever once doing that.

I walked back to my house, where my husband was making

tacos for dinner. (Those yellow kits can be a lifesaver when you're starving and out of meal ideas.)

"That was weird," I told him, then recounted the whole conversation.

"Are you going to run?" he asked. "Is that something you'd actually want to do?"

"No," I said, because it wasn't something I could even imagine doing. "But someone should."

Over tacos, I mentioned running for the county board to the kids, who looked at me blankly.

"Would I have to do anything?" my daughter asked.

"Not really," I said. "I just won't be home as much."

"Cool," she said. "So, are you going to do it?"

"No," I said. "But someone should."

My intention was to email Dave the next day and politely decline. I didn't have the first inkling of how to run for office, much less what the office entailed. Surely, someone else was more qualified. I know the county government is responsible for . . . something? Snow plows, maybe? Definitely not schools, because they have their own separate board. And definitely not trash removal, because we pay a private company for that. So, snowplowing and . . . maybe the jail?

What with one thing and another—the attempted repeal of Obamacare was happening in DC at the same time—a week or two went by before I got around to emailing Dave. And thus the idea had time to percolate in the back of my brain.

I was, in fact, qualified, if only because I gave enough of a damn to learn what I knew I didn't know—which was what I'd been doing since January, when I became deeply invested in the workings of the federal government in a way I'd never imagined possible. If I can get up to speed on "cloture" and the "Hastert rule," I thought, I sure as heck can figure out how snowplows work.

Then there was my memory of the Women's March. Did that ocean of pink suddenly make me feel like a warrior? Of course not. But it did assure me that at least a few of those women would have my back and were counting on me not to let our side down. If nothing else, funneling my energy into running for office would bleed off some rage.

Besides, the absolute worst possible outcome for me was that I would put time into a campaign and lose. At most, I'd be out a couple hundred dollars for yard signs and flyers. My family and friends would still love and (mostly) tolerate me. My community standing would go from "that lady who used to write stories about her kids for the local paper" to "that lady who ran for the county board and lost" (if anyone in the community even thought about me at all, mind, which is debatable).

Whenever I think about trying anything new, I always run the worst-case scenario. It's a twitch I picked up after my first few years as a writer. When you are trying to make a living with words, you get used to hearing "no." If you can't embrace losing, you won't last long. Losing is part of the game. You check off the "no" box and move to the next potential "yes." It's not personal. Hearing voters say "no" would be just another day.

It was the idea of spending my own money on the venture that was harder to justify. I'd been squirreling cash away for an exotic family vacation before our eldest went to college, a deadline that was flying toward us faster every minute. If we trimmed our expectations a bit, we could do our part to save the republic by going to Montreal rather than Paris. I've heard the *Mona Lisa* is less impressive in person, anyway.

What finally sold me on freeing up the Benjamins is a conversation I had with Gary, who'd been on the board for a few years. The cost would be a few yard signs and maybe a newspaper ad, he told me. Races in very small counties have financial stakes in the hundreds, not the thousands, he said. I therefore limited myself to spending eight hundred dollars of my own money. Anything else would need to come from other people, which meant I'd need to ask other people, which was a bridge I'd cross if and when I had to.

I decided that eight hundred dollars was a small price to pay to give the Republican incumbent a signal that he couldn't just keep his position without working a little bit. If nothing else, running against him would be a small nod to my pink-hatted sisters. I could #Resist by throwing some sand in the gears of my representative's march to victory. He wouldn't get to win by default again, and it was pretty clear that I was the only one willing to step in the way.

Now, in case you're waiting for some small-town dirt on my opponent, know that you won't be getting any. As far as I know, he's a decent guy who loves his family. He grew up here, and I did not, which means that our social circles don't overlap that much. Still, his kids go to the same orthodontist as mine. I know which of the businesses he or his extended family owns. I have friends who go to the same synagogue he does. There aren't even two degrees of separation between us because this is a small town.

His son and my son are in the same grade, and that fact has made open houses at the middle school awkward, especially given that our kids have had a couple of classes together. But there will be no great hair-pulling, trash-talking scene in the middle of Parents' Night in the Earth Science classroom. No one will flip a table and yell, "Filthy whore." If that's what you want, prepare for disappointment.

Still, this is a small town. There is no end of gossip. I've heard rumors about him; I'm sure he's heard rumors about me (all of which are true, by the way, including the one about the pirate). But one of the hazards of running for office in a small town is that anything you say about someone will get back to that person. Without fail, you will then wind up face-to-face with the human you trash-talked in the grocery store or the dentist's office. And I'm not willing to live a life where I can't look someone in the eye without being crippled by shame.

Besides, my choice to run had nothing to do with what I thought of him and his personal life. His official choices on the county board, however, could have been more supportive of those in our community who needed our help. I did not feel that the policies he'd endorsed represented what our part of the city would also have endorsed had they been paying more attention.

Yes, I wanted him off the board because he was a Republican at a time when that party's leader was a grabby grifter and that ethos had trickled down. Or maybe it had trickled up. The shift to a certain kind of Republican rule, one more concerned with women's bodies and bathrooms, had slowly suffused local and state governments for about a decade. And it hit our county board in 2015, when voters swung hard for the Republicans and we had only four Democrats among its fourteen members. In the last two years, progress on increasing the number of decent jobs in the county or preparing for an increasingly unpredictable climate had ground to a halt.

Once I began paying attention, I found the board's unwillingness to do much of anything beyond the mandated necessities galling. Shifting the balance of power even a tiny bit had the potential to shift the county's way of thinking and, maybe, get us moving on promoting green energy, investigating some hinky business in the Sheriff's Office, and paying county employees enough to live on.

Ultimately, none of that is what made up my mind to run. It was more instinctive than anything else. My anger simply pushed me over the edge. It threatened to boil over every time I looked at my phone or opened the newspaper or, frankly, breathed. Merely sitting on my couch waiting for the next hit of outrage and horror coming out of DC was changing nothing but my own blood pressure. I woke up every morning feeling like I'd swallowed rocks during the night and they had been grinding away for hours on end. Later on, I'd discover that I'd developed irritable bowel syndrome. The less said about its symptoms, the better.

All my repressed ire and unrelenting fear was starting to have a real impact on my body, clearly, but it was also doing a number on my psyche. My irrational fear of flying, which plagued my early twenties even though I know exactly how physics works, came roaring back in the middle of a flight to see my mom in Florida. Thirty-thousand feet is really not the best height at which to start hyperventilating and sweating. Can I blame all my woes on the Trump regime? Or was all this going to happen anyway when I made the transition from my mid-forties to my almost-fifties? Hard to say.

So, I made the choice to be proactive rather than reactive and run for the District Twelve seat on the Otsego County Board.

CHAPTER 5

The Confidence of a Middle-Aged White Guy

In an ideal world, I'd give you a detailed checklist of what you have to do to run for a local government office. There would be an order to it and little boxes you could put stickers in when you'd performed each task.

That is not going to happen. First, a bunch of items all needed to happen concurrently, which screws up a numbered list. But, mostly, all local offices are just a little bit different. What you need to do for New York's Otsego County will be different from what you need to do in Michigan's Otsego County. Even within New York State, the requirements change. Cayuga is different from Tioga, which is different from Onondaga. The five New York City boroughs have their own sets of arcane government structures that don't resemble the rest of the state's, because organizing eight million people on 469 square miles requires a more convoluted structure, I guess. Still, broad generalizations can be made. You will need to collect signatures, raise money, and knock on doors.

Local offices (county boards, city councils, town aldermen) are everywhere, and they actually have much more control over daily life than the splashier federal offices. While the ban on transgender people in the military is important, it's important in a diffuse way, unless you yourself are one of the estimated six thousand transgender people in the military. The number of people directly harmed by this misguided, boneheaded edict is relatively small, even if the indirect outrage over the injustice is broad.

Compare that to the number of people who live where they might have an encounter with common North American fauna, such as raccoons, possums, deer, and bats. Said fauna can carry rabies. If you're bitten by one of them, which happens more than you'd think, your local health department can tell you whether you should worry about foaming at the mouth. This is to say nothing of the ticks that can live on said common fauna and that enjoy spreading some highly unpleasant diseases. Thirty thousand people contract Lyme disease each year from tick bites, and that number is likely higher because it's one of those conditions that is underdiagnosed.

Every year, hundreds of thousands of Americans are poisoned by their food or by the lead in their water or the radon in their basements. Every year, the flu takes out a nontrivial number of us. Yes, our country's stance on transgender people or a border wall or North Korea is important, but these are not the biggest hazards in our immediate environments. The fact that we have the time to worry about Kim Jong-un's nukes rather than a fatal flu strain is proof that our county health departments, which are responsible for mitigating mundane hazards, are doing a pretty good job.

Again, I'm in no way implying that the posture the federal government takes toward nonwhite, nonstraight, nonmale communities isn't important. But what might have a more immediate impact is what's going on in your own community among the people you know.

Take my county, which has one of the leading centers for

transgender wellness in the northeastern United States, the Susquehanna Family Practice and Gender Wellness Center. Patients drive here from big cities like Albany and remote areas such as the North Country. In 2016, the *Guardian* ran a feature on its founder, Dr. Carolyn Wolf-Gould. She and her husband, Chris, ran a standard family practice in the area for years. In 2007, Carolyn was approached by Toni Blessing, a trans patient who needed a refill on his testosterone prescription. He called Carolyn to ask if she'd be his doctor. She remembers replying, "I can't be your doctor. I don't know anything about it. Blah, blah, blah, blah."

His response was, "Well, I can't go to Philadelphia all the time."

"I took him as a patient, and then trained," Carolyn says. "Slowly, the practice has grown. We've served over seven hundred transgender medical patients and over three hundred transgender mental health patients. Right now, we're getting about a hundred fifty new transgender patients a year."

The Gender Wellness Center now does everything from primary care to family therapy as well as community-based research and legal advocacy. Plus, it offers some of the basic gender-affirming surgeries. "Not the fancy ones," Carolyn says, "but the basic ones—and we do a lot of training and education for doctors and community members."

For Carolyn, doing this work is not only about the actual medicine. "I'm very committed to social justice in my life" she says. "This is a way to combine my practice with social justice. The stigma and horrible discrimination people face—it's just appalling. So, when people come to us, they are so pleased to get care. It's just really, really, really rewarding. Many of the people who come to me are very healthy. It's a different model for care—going to the doctor to learn how to find your authentic self. I would just say it is an incredible privilege to bear witness to the process of unfolding. There's just nothing like it."

It's the beauty of the process that makes the hard parts (such as figuring out how to pay for all of it) worthwhile. The center is able to expand its services and reach further into the community because of private grants and other forms of public funding. Some of the support comes through the U.S. Department of Health, some through a state program known as DSRIP (which is redesigning the state's Medicaid system), which is administered on a local level, and from a private grant from the Robert Wood Johnson Foundation. But beyond these direct sources, many of Carolyn's clients rely on more than forty community programs, many of which are funded in part by the county as well.

If any of those local systems were cut, the center would have a much harder time serving all its clients' needs and would be forced to focus only on what insurance paid for—which, frankly, isn't much. Carolyn told the *Guardian* that figuring out "hormones isn't rocket science. The hardest part of all of this is the paperwork, from insurance companies with systems that aren't designed to account for trans procedures."

Usually, a center like Wolf-Gould's would be in a big city with a high concentration of LGBTQ people, "but most of the country isn't a big city," Carolyn says. "We're trying to design a model that can be used in other places. A South Dakota family practice could do something like we're doing, so we're trying to create a center here and create a model by embedding the care in a family practice."

So, yes, fighting against a ban on transgender people in the military is important, but fighting to ensure that local health services for trans people remain comprehensive probably has a bigger impact where you live, even if it is a small city in the middle of nowhere. Protecting these programs is also important, and they are also under siege.

That's not to imply that these local systems are perfect—even with the best health department, people still get Lyme disease and rabies—but imagine how many more people in your neighborhood would be sick if the local health department didn't exist.

What I've just discussed only begins to outline what these stolid and dedicated workers do. I haven't even mentioned the car seats or the vaccines or the biological terrorism emergency plans. (Personally, I try not to dwell on the biological terrorism plans, other than to rest assured that they exist.)

While national offices suck all the oxygen out of the room, local offices are where the rubber meets the road—in fact, they're tasked with maintaining that road so the rubber can meet it. These local government positions are in every cranny of the country. According to Amanda Litman, one of the founders of the progressive candidate support organization Run for Something, "There are more elected offices in the country than there are McDonald's employees."

These are the positions that have a direct impact on your quality of life, and yet, historically (if we take historically to mean recent decades in history), no one wants to fight for them. Forty percent of local seats, which will have a huge impact on redistricting in 2020, went uncontested in 2016. Just think of the impact you could have in one of those seats. As Hillary Clinton said to Litman (even before the Supreme Court left the fate of the nation in the hands of those willing to run for local office and fight against partisan gerrymandering), "Change doesn't always come from Washington, DC. It can come from your local school board or city council. In fact, most of the progress we're seeing right now is happening on a local level. Policy ideas we worked on and fought for during the campaign are taking hold in cities and states across the country—like New York, which recently became the first state in the nation to make public college tuition-free for working families." (Not to toot my own state's horn—lord knows we're obnoxious enough—but she was talking about the Excelsior Scholarship program. It's really an innovative policy and something that my own kids will likely take advantage of.)

True progress can be made if we "focus on the offices that actually get shit done: state legislatures, city councils, school boards, and mayorships. Look at who's leading the resistance: the local officials who truly understand their communities," Litman says. And she's not wrong.

Look at Danica Roem, the transgender woman who defeated a Republican incumbent for a seat in the Virginia House of Delegates in 2017. Roem won because she focused her energy on a problem that her community faced: traffic. (Her gender identity wasn't part of her argument.) Now she's put herself in a position to make a tangible, measurable change in her neighbors' lives.

This is why political systems developed in the first place: it is easier to solve problems that plague the group as a group. In a representational democracy, we elect people to represent our group's interests. In theory, this works. In practice, however, there are flaws. One of the biggest ones was evident right from the start. In 1776, Abigail Adams wrote to her husband, John, who was then in the throes of drafting the Declaration of Independence with four other white guys, "Be more generous and favorable to [women] than your ancestors," she wrote. "Do not put such unlimited power into the hands of the husbands. . . . If particular care and attention is not paid to the ladies, we are determined to foment a rebellion, and will not hold ourselves bound by any laws in which we have no voice, or representation."

We know now how that turned out. It would take another 144 years for women to earn the right to vote and longer still for them to occupy elected offices in significant numbers. The suffrage movement started before the Civil War, as women chafed at the idea of the Cult of True Womanhood, which rigidly defined a woman's role as subservient helpmeet. Susan B. Anthony, whose face would eventually grace a one-dollar coin, got her start not far from my house.

Anthony had gone to a Sons of Temperance meeting in Albany in 1852. The evening was characterized by men standing up to talk at length about how women drove them to drink and/or explaining to the women present what alcohol was (I'm guessing). Anthony stood up to speak as well—at which point, she was told to sit down because "the sisters were not invited to speak, but to listen and learn." It's funny (for relative values of "funny") how little can change in 167 years.

While the Civil War was in the fighting-and-dying stage, women's rights took a backseat to the horrors on the front. After the war, women balked at freed male slaves being given the franchise before white women were—yes, even progressives can be racist—and this racism would split the suffrage movement in two.

As the 1900s churned on, suffragists endured physical violence, including forced feedings, to further their cause. Suffragist Lucy Burns was chained to a cell wall with her hands above her head and left there. Another woman was thrown into her cell, where she thwacked her head on a metal bed and was knocked unconscious. Another was thrown repeatedly over an iron bench; others were kicked, punched, and choked by guards. After newspapers began reporting this brutal treatment, public sentiment started to sway. Finally, the Nineteenth Amendment, after a nail-biter of a vote in Tennessee, the last state needed to ratify it, was signed in 1920.

Even after all that, the "women's vote" failed to really change much in terms of who got elected. Only one-third of women eligible to vote did so in the 1920 election. And most of those who did, writes Elaine Weiss in *The Woman's Hour: The Great Fight to Win the Vote*, tended to vote as their husbands did. Meanwhile, the Ku Klux Klan kept black women from the polls in South Carolina. In Ocoee, Florida, in 1920, fifty black men and women were killed in Election Day violence. Even now, one hundred-plus years on from the amendments that applied the franchise equally to all citizens, the right to vote is still unevenly distributed. As with the livestock in Orwell's *Animal Farm*, some people are more equal than others.

The image of my foremothers being beaten for wanting to cast a ballot is one of the reasons I have voted at every opportunity, in big elections and small. Still, despite my love of exercising my franchise, the idea of running for office had never occurred to me.

I'm certain I'm not the only woman who hasn't ever thought about public office, especially in the years leading up to 2018, when record numbers of my gender were voted into positions up and down the ballot. Before that watershed, the women who held office seemed hyperconfident and incredibly knowledgeable, which are two states I couldn't even dream of achieving in the realm of public policy. While I noticed how smart these women were, I failed to notice how a mediocre white man could bumble his way into office on the strength of charm and self-regard.

Still, men were in the political sphere long before women even thought to enter it. We women took longer to run for office because we weren't permitted in most public spaces. Remember, we couldn't enter the workforce, really, until the Second World War, and once the men returned from the front lines, we were informed that it was time for us to go back to home and hearth. And a great many women did just that. A smaller number of women, whether it was because their husbands, sons, or fathers hadn't come back or because they simply liked it, kept bringing home the proverbial bacon—at which point, things being what they were, we would have to cook it and clean up afterward.

The cultural shifts of the early 1960s saw the publication of *The Feminine Mystique* (1963) and the formation of the National Organization for Women (1966). In 1964, Maine Republican Margaret Chase was the first woman (post-Nineteenth Amendment) to make a major bid for the U.S. presidency. Eight years later, New York Democrat Shirley Chisholm became the first black woman of a major party to do the same. Geraldine Ferraro ran for vice president on the ticket with Walter Mondale in 1984; and in 2008, Sarah Palin did the same for John McCain.

As for legislative positions, until the 1970s, the number of women who served in the federal government could comfortably fit in a small movie theater. Most of the women in those seats were appointed to fill out their husbands' terms rather than elected by their constituents. In 1978, Kansas Republican Nancy Kassebaum won her place in the U.S. Senate in a regular election. By 1979, women occupied fewer than 5 percent of the seats in the U.S. House. With those sorts of numbers, it's no wonder that a dedicated bathroom for female House members wasn't installed until the 1960s and the Senate had no ladies' room until the 1990s.

The gender divide is especially resistant to change when it comes to elected office. While roughly 58 percent of American workers are female, women make up only 19 percent of Congress, 24 percent of state legislatures, 33 percent of city councils in Top 100 cities, and 18.2 percent of mayors of Top 100 cities.

Women aren't anywhere near parity when it comes to representation in government, which doesn't make it a shocker that we don't even think of running in the first place. During the last fifteen years, political scientists Jennifer Lawless and Richard Fox have dived deep into the political pool. Through studies of "lawyers, business leaders, educators and political activists," they write in *Women, Men and U.S. Politics: Ten Big Questions*, "We can determine whether women and men—all else equal—have similar ambition to run for office. Long story short: they don't."

Lawless and Fox's data indicate that men are roughly 17 percent more likely to run for office in general. When it comes to a state office, men are 40 percent more likely; for a federal position, they are twice as likely. If my sex were different, I likely would have thought about running for office much sooner.

There is a temptation to blame every obstacle faced by women on the patriarchy. Yet, in this case, it appears that that blame is well placed. Like the manicurist Madge said in the Palmolive ad, we're soaking in it. The deep-seated conditioning we've all undergone just by growing up in a place where women are seen as lesser than their male cohorts is one of the reasons Hillary Clinton lost in 2016. Parts of the electorate, both men and women, just couldn't imagine a person with two X chromosomes in the Oval Office, no matter how qualified she was to be there.

It's a message that starts early. As Fox and Lawless explain,

"Researchers have found that, from as early as elementary school, boys are taught to be confident, assertive, and self-promoting. Girls often receive the message—if even only subtly—that it is inappropriate or undesirable to posses these characteristics. As a result, from a young age, women are more likely than men to exhibit a tendency to diminish and under-value their skills and achievements."

Or, to put it succinctly, give every woman the confidence of a middle-class white guy, and we'll run the world.

What Lawless and Fox have also discovered is that once the decision to run is made, women and men perform about the same in elections. There isn't a penalty in the ballot box for being female until you start to look at big federal offices. The harder part, however, is getting a woman on the ballot in the first place.

"Women are less likely to run without being prodded," Litman explains. "Countless academic studies show that we underestimate our abilities and assume we need to be even more qualified than men in order to run for office, or apply for that job, or raise our hand to speak."

All that being said, the political landscape changed in 2016. We thought we were about to see the first female president. Instead, we are seeing millions of women rise up, run, and win. If Trump can be president, anything is possible.

Lawless and Fox put it this way: "Nonprofit organizations opposed to Trump's agenda have seen a surge in donations. And organizations that recruit and train women to run for office report a record number of applicants. As one woman who decided she wants to run for a county or state legislative seat in New Jersey said, 'The election was a kick in the pants that I had to step up and be more involved.'"

Let's revisit EMILY's List, a PAC that works to get pro-

choice Democratic women elected. In 2017, EMILY's List saw
the number of women asking for their help boom. According
to *Time* magazine, "the group had to knock down a wall in its
Washington office to make room for more staff."

As CNN points out, "In 1970, there was just one female
Senate candidate. [In 2018], there are 49 to 54 women running,
depending on whether and which third-party candidates you
include. There are 394 women running for the House and 56
in governor's races (including third-party candidates), as of
May 23, 2018."

Politico cautiously dubbed 2018 "The Year of the Woman."
The sheer number of women who ran and won that year
was greater than the country saw during the last "Year of the
Woman," in 1992, following Anita Hill's testimony before Congress on now-Supreme Court justice Clarence Thomas's sexual
harassment.

The 2018 version looks like a tsunami by comparison. From
the #MeToo movement to the record number of women winning political office, to say nothing of the ongoing shifts in how
We the People manage power and race, we are in the middle
of figuring out what our country is and what we should strive
to be. It's a conversation that has been a long time coming and
that, at times (as in the case of Charlottesville, Virginia, in
2017), has turned violent.

The 2018 midterm elections proved that real change is
under way. According to 2018 numbers from EMILY's List,
more than 26,000 women contacted the PAC for information
about running for office; during the 2016 election cycle, that
number was 920.

In 2018, women won more than 90 seats in the U.S. House.
Two of those are held by the first Muslim women to sit in that
body. Iowa elected its first female member of Congress. Ten-

nessee voted in its first female senator; Massachusetts has its first black U.S. House rep. The first Native Americans to hold House seats came from Kansas and New Mexico.

The recent trend away from straight, white male candidates ran true on the state level as well, with Maine electing its first female governor and Colorado its first openly gay male one. Women have made a hard push for the 2020 presidential ticket, with Kamala Harris, Kirsten Gillibrand, Elizabeth Warren, Amy Klobuchar, Marianne Williamson, and Tulsi Gabbard all announcing their intentions. By now, dear reader, you know more than I do about who remains in the race. For the record, my sincerest hope is that a woman still has a shot at the top job.

"It would be foolish to make too much of any one race," says Jean Sinzdak, associate director of Rutgers University's Center for American Women and Politics. "But all of this together— there's something going on right now."

On a national level, Trump triggered an avalanche of diversity in those seeking office. It is an easy trend to spot, now that we're a couple of years out, but the first visible sign of the estrogen wave happened less than twenty-four hours after his inauguration, just as those of us not on the Trump train were searching for footing after a bananas inaugural address and a spittle-filled rant by his (first) press secretary, Sean Spicer.

Kristi Andersen, a professor emeritus at the Maxwell School at Syracuse University and a member of the Cazenovia (New York) Town Board, has spent her career and beyond thinking about women running for office. "Basically, the story is mostly that women and girls are not socialized to think about politics as a possible avocation as much as boys. And they don't think of themselves as qualified," she says. "I think, in a simplistic way, educated women, black and white, were just so upset, pissed off, and discouraged after the 2016 election that this got a lot of them past this notion that 'This is not something I should be doing,' or 'Somebody else will do this,' or 'Well, it's not that important.' All those arguments against doing this were washed away."

That's why I ran: It dawned on me that I could, and I had run out of arguments not to.

CHAPTER 6

How to Get on the Ballot

Once you've made up your mind to do so, the first step in running for office is getting your name on the ballot. Every state has a different process for this. In none of the states is it as easy as simply calling the Board of Elections and asking nicely—which is a bummer.

In New York State, getting on the ballot requires collecting signatures from a percentage of those you'd be representing. That number is determined by the state's Board of Elections. For offices such as governor, you need to collect at least fifteen thousand signatures. For local offices, the numbers can range from a few hundred to fewer than ten. The number also varies depending on which party's line you are trying to run on, if that party agrees to let you run there, and/or if you want to run as an independent.

Independent, by the way, should never be confused with *Independence*, which is a political party in its own right. Fun fact: a lot of New Yorkers who check the "Independence" box when registering think they are now officially "Independent." Instead, what they've done is join a very small conservative party. True independents shouldn't check any boxes for party and will show up on the voter rolls as "BLK," which means they left the party box blank.

When we start talking about political parties, shit gets weird. You know about the two biggest, Republicans and Democrats, but there are a bunch of others that have a large enough membership to make an impact. On the more conservative end of the continuum, we have the Conservative, Independence (not Independent), and Reform Parties. On the liberal end, we have the Green, Women's Equality, and Working Families Parties.

This isn't to say that some of the smaller concerns, such as the Communist, Labor, Right to Life, and Workers World Parties, don't run candidates in the state. They just don't tend to run where I am. We do have a very young Libertarian— during the 2017 race he wasn't old enough to drink legally— who keeps making a run at office, if only to make a point, Ron Swanson–style, about how government should do nothing but fund the military. This is fine, but I do wonder if his views will change once he experiences a little bit more of the world.

In New York, if you are registered with a party, you can be on its line on the ballot if you collect the required number of signatures, which is 5 percent of the people registered in that district in that party. If more than one person in one party does this before the deadline, there will be a primary. If not, that name carries over to the general.

Fairly straightforward, yes? Just wait.

If you would also like to run on another party's line, you can collect the required number of signatures and ask that party for permission to represent it. It's a good idea to do this, if you can. First, running on more than one party line increases the real estate your name takes up on the ballot. Second, there are some staunch single-party voters who will never, ever cast their ballot for a member of a party they hate but will vote for the exact same person if that person has any other party attached to his or her name.

For example, a Democratic loyalist would never dream of voting for Johanna Smith (R) because it would signal support for the party of Roger Stone. However, that same voter is free to vote for Johanna Smith (C), for Conservative, because that shows support for the party of . . . um . . . James L. Buckley, a U.S. senator from 1971–77. (Yes, I had to google it.)

It is possible to run on both the Democratic and Republican lines, and this has happened more than once in my county over the last couple of years. For example, in the 2018 sheriff's race—yes, we elect our sheriffs in these parts—the Republican incumbent faced a challenger who was a registered Republican, which meant he could force a primary. However, said challenger also asked to run on the Democrats' line, which meant that he would still be on the final ballot even if he lost the primary. Given how unpopular the incumbent was, the Democrats said, "Whatever it takes to get this guy out of office," and let a lifelong Republican run as a Democrat when he lost the primary. The incumbent kept his office, by the way, and the whole Republican-as-Democrat switcheroo roiled the local party for a few days. Pragmatists pointed fingers at the die-hard moralists, while the moderates pointedly looked at the ceiling and whistled tunelessly. There isn't that much space between family dynamics and intraparty dynamics, frankly, and the middle children always get the fuzzy end of the stick, which is fine if everyone would just stop fighting already.

The independent (not Independence) line only adds to the mayhem. Anyone can run as an independent, as long as they collect the required number of signatures. As an independent, you can also name your own party, if you are so inclined. So, you could be an independent running for the "Cheese Is Amazing" Party, which has one member, which is you.

Confused yet? Buckle up. We're about to talk about signatures.

Signatures can be collected only during designated weeks in the election calendar. Any collected before or after the official dates will be tossed out. If you are running for an established party line, you have one set of dates. If you are an independent, you have a different set of dates.

Good so far, yes?

Signatures are collected on a "designating petition," which you download from the state's website. Make sure you use the right-size paper when you print it; otherwise, your signatures can be thrown out. If you are running on a party line, only the signatures from members of that party count. If you are running on an independent line, signatures from any voter of any party count, but only if that voter hasn't already signed another ballot. If there are two people running for the same position from the same party, a signatory can sign only one person's petition. If he or she signs both, then neither signature counts. The signer's address also goes on the petition, and if there are mistakes there and/or part of the address is illegible, the signature can be thrown out. If the person writes "city" in the "Town or City" box when they actually live in the town, the signature can be thrown out. If the date is wrong—say you accidentally write "4/17/18" when it was actually "4/17/17," even if a logical person would assume you didn't collect a signature from the future—the signature can be thrown out. And if you screw up the bottom part of the page, which is all about who witnessed what when (and is far too tedious to go into here), an entire page of signatures can be thrown out.

But how are they thrown out?

That is a good question, imaginary inquisitor. The opposing party has a few days during which it can challenge any signature on your petition once you've turned it in. But does that actually happen?

Another fine question! It's as if you're a mind reader!

For the county board seat, this last happened in 2015, when the signatures on Democrat Andrew Marietta's petition were contested by the Republican incumbent. Mud was flung, and the whole issue wound up in court. From the *Cooperstown Crier*:

> "The difference between Democrats and Republicans is we look to count every signature and they look to knock out every signature," [Democratic chairman Rich] Abbate said, noting one challenge is aimed at 2015 Cooperstown graduate Patrick Dewey, who has cerebral palsy who uses a stamp for his signature.
>
> Otsego County Republican Chairman Vince Casale said state election law does not allow stamps to be used on petitions and contended the petitions turned in on behalf of Marietta are marred by a host of irregularities.
>
> "His petitions were all a mess," Casale said. "He didn't get the required number of valid signatures."

Newsflash: The New York State Supreme Court ruled that Marietta had obtained the required number of signatures. Despite Casale's move to block the Democrat from the ballot, Marietta not only took his legally justified place there, but also won the election. He's been on the board since 2015.

This isn't an isolated incident. Sometimes, questioning a signature's validity uncovers intentional fraud, as it did in 2018, in a statehouse race where a Republican candidate's staffer decided to forge a few signatures and hope no one noticed. Yet, mostly, these challenges don't expose felonies. What they frequently expose is poor handwriting and cynical partisan hackery.

Every election cycle, the signature petitions are scrutinized by actors for all parties who are just looking for enough nit-picky procedural mistakes to boot an otherwise viable candidate off the ballot. I waver between being okay with this (after all, details are important when you're handling the public's business) and finding it fantastically irritating (after all, we should find ways to get more people on the ballot rather than fewer). Plus, a lot of the rules about signatures rely on strangers telling you the truth about or remembering what they've signed, which—let's be honest—has a fifty-fifty shot of working out.

Still, this is the system we have, and we just have to work with it until we can change it. (And that, Dear Reader, sums up government, more or less.)

⊙ ⊙ ⊙

My introduction to this whole process took place during "candidate school," a course offered by the Otsego County Democratic Committee, which gives a quick-and-dirty overview of how the ballot process works. Our candidate school took place in a local "athletic club" that was less about participating in athletic endeavors than watching them. It's a bar, basically, and one with a back room where I'd attended more than one kid's birthday party. This is how we roll in Otsego County. Civic functions are treated with reverence and draft beer.

Our instructor was the Democrat-affiliated county commissioner of elections, who walked us through a PowerPoint presentation on the dos and don'ts. (There is also a Republican-affiliated county commissioner of elections, by the way. I assume she did the same for her party's candidates.)

As a result of how contentious signatures are, we were instructed to collect at least 150 percent more than we needed. (Really, best practices encourage twice as many as you need, but half again as many will work if you enjoy taking risks.)

There was the briefest of overviews about campaign finance laws and the Freedom of Information Act. Fortunately, my past career as a newspaper reporter and not-as-past career teaching Communication Law gave me a leg up on FOIA. Campaign finance law would later kick my heinie, but that was a hurdle I'd yet to crash into.

Apart from learning what constituted a "signature," I also learned that Otsego County elected its coroners, and that anyone can run for coroner if he or she has an urge to do so. So, if the whole Board of Representatives thing didn't work out, I could be the person who shows up and says, "Yup. Dead." The thought makes me want to barf in a bucket, and the implication that any goober like me could hold this job remains unsettling.

Armed with knowledge and motivated by fear, on June 6, 2017, I printed out my petitions and started collecting signatures. I was required to find 24 (really, between 36 and 48, once you factor in a cushion) humans registered with the Democratic Party in my district who were willing to give me a shot. The entire district has 880-ish people. The Board of Elections provided a voter list. Easy enough, I thought. I probably know at least 36 who are Democrats.

Getting to double digits was a snap. The first two to sign were my husband and my father, who lives across the street. Dave, the guy who'd pulled me into this whole project, and his wife were willing to sign, too. So were John and Jenny, our first (and best) friends from when we'd moved here fourteen years before. I was on a roll.

I couldn't sign my own petition, by the way, because then I couldn't also witness it, which would have made the whole thing invalid. It also feels like cheating. And in any case, *of course* I thought I should be in office.

I picked up a couple of signatures after church, which is totally legal even if it feels like it shouldn't be. Also, we're Unitarian Universalists, so it would be more accurate to call it a vaguely spiritual gathering followed by coffee. In no time, I was up to 15, and had run out of potential signers I already knew.

It's not that I don't know more than fifteen people, mind you. I mean, I'm not a regular cocktail party habitué, but I do leave my house every now and again. No, as it turns out, most of the people I've met in my decade and a half living here either don't live in my district or aren't registered with a party. (One person who lives in the district wasn't registered to vote at all, but I will not name him and he's since rectified the situation. Still, how hard is it for a full-grown adult human to do the bare minimum that a full-grown adult human should? I'll bet he also doesn't return his shopping cart to the cart corral, the true test of whether one is a full-grown adult human who should be allowed to live in civilization.)

When I started this running-for-office journey, I knew I'd have to go door to door eventually. But now the moment had come. I had to knock on doors.

Every voter should hear your message, everyone told me, ideally more than once. There were two problems with this: first, I didn't have a message, other than "I need to channel my anger," and second, knocking on a stranger's door gives me the willies. Even as a child on Halloween, I found the idea of bothering someone at home spooky enough to keep me from hauling in pounds of sweet loot.

My message, I decided, could be a problem for another day, one that might not come if I couldn't collect enough signatures to get myself on the ballot. If anyone asked, I figured it would be enough to say that I was running because I thought the race should be competitive and that the incumbent didn't just get to have it. No one ever did ask, which is good, because that message is terrible.

I chose a sunny Saturday afternoon in June, put on a skirt and top that made me look like a responsible adult, chucked my petition clipboard and voter list in a tote bag, and set out. I figured I could pick up the remaining signatures I needed and be home by dinner.

Here is what I learned over the span of four hours:

- Knocking on doors never gets easy, but it does get less hard.
- You will spend more time answering questions about why you are asking people to sign rather than why you are running in the first place.
- Dogs generally like you; cats do not.
- You will be asked to hold a baby, haul a heavy box into the foyer, and find a pair of reading glasses—though, not all for the same person.
- Clearly marked house numbers are not a priority for every home owner; nor are safe front steps, or visible doorbells.
- At more than one house, you will wonder if this is where you will have a handkerchief doused with chloroform slapped over your mouth as you're dragged into a basement.
- Only the foolish fail to carry water on a sunny June afternoon, and you are a fool.
- One homeowner, whom you never see, will tell you to go away because everyone in the house has tuberculosis, which can't possibly be true, but whatever.
- You will spend more than a little time wondering how people would respond if you were anything other than a tall, roundish, gray-haired white woman.

- On sunny Saturday afternoons in June, half the town is elsewhere.

That last bit was the sticky part. For every person I talked to, five weren't home, which sucked up a lot of the time I'd allotted myself. After four sweaty hours walking around the two dozen or so blocks of what I'd started to think of as "my" district, I gave up and headed home with only ten more signatures on my petition.

◦ ◦ ◦

In an ideal world, there would have been some kind of checklist for newbies running for office in 2017. There are some good ones now, such as the ones provided by Amanda Litman of Run for Something, a nonprofit organization that aims to recruit and support young, diverse progressives to run for down-ballot races in order to build a bench for the future. The checklist provided by Run for Something does a great job of explaining how anything is possible now that Trump is president and shows you exactly what you need to know before you jump in. Such resources were thin when I took this on.

Instead, most of my campaign, such as it was, was guided by the Democrats who'd run for similar lowly local offices, and most of their counsel was earnest but not terribly helpful. At least half of them had strolled into office unopposed and merely shrugged when I asked them how to run against an incumbent. The other half, including the former (and only) female mayor of Oneonta, Kim Muller, kept it simple: talk to as many constituents as you can.

I'd dropped by Kim's house, a three-minute walk from mine, to get her signature on my petition. While she's out of the mayor game, Muller is still "public service adjacent," working as a consultant for state agencies to increase educational services for immigrants. And because she's a decent person (and really wanted a Democrat back in the seat), she asked how the signature collecting was going. I groused about the tedium of knocking on doors and giving my spiel. And again, because she's a decent person, she didn't just shake her head and say, "Oh, honey. You don't even know what real tedium is. Just wait until you're in office." Instead, she gave me a little pep talk, signed my form, and sent me on my way.

While past me was out collecting signatures again, present me was thinking that Kim had real wisdom to share about women in office, even if she wasn't currently occupying a seat in the public sector. She knows how the game is played but always seems optimistic that sanity will eventually win out. I knew I needed to meet with her again and really pick her brains.

Kim launched her political career from a District Twelve County Board seat (yes, the very same one I was running for), and though more than thirty years had elapsed between our campaigns—she started in 1985—not much had changed since then.

"I ran for county board because I moved here from DC," she says. "I worked on Maryland's Paul Sarbanes campaign for reelection to the U.S. Senate. I got very involved in the environment issues because I worked for the Interior Department under James Watt."

We're sitting on a bench in her eponymous square on a warm spring day. The initial plan was to meet for coffee at the local Latte Lounge, which is just around the corner from the brick-paved Muller Plaza. We wandered outside not because I wanted a poetic moment of interviewing her in her square, but because, after such a long winter, both of us wanted to restore our vitamin D reserves. A fiction writer could never get away with a scene where two women talk politics in a public place named after one of them, and yet, there we were.

"I moved here, and I was like, 'I want to run for office,'" Kim says. "And the head of the county party said, 'Democrats don't run for office here.' I said, 'Well, I want to. I've got to make a difference.' I was twenty-eight years old, I had a kid, and I was in this town."

In the county's two-hundred-plus-year history, Muller was only the second woman to serve on the board. The first, Democrat Frances Waddington, had been elected a few years before.

"It was an old boy network," Kim says. "They would literally go in the bathroom to talk. And, literally, they would tell really gross jokes. They were horrendous on that level and very chauvinistic. Plus, I was a very strong Dem, and they were Republicans."

One of the ways Kim worked through the network was to practically memorize *Robert's Rules of Order*, and to challenge the rest of the board and the county attorney when they wouldn't let her speak. "I wasn't even always right," she admits, "but I knew the rules better than they did, so I could give them a hard time."

It was still hard, however. "Representative Joe Kenyon came across a desk. I thought he was going to punch me—and he was a *Democrat*. They just couldn't handle being challenged."

This gender divide might be why one of Kim's best friends is Kathy Clark, a Republican board member who was the board chair in 2015. No matter their political differences, the two leaned on each other because they were the odd women out. Each helped raise the other's children, and they are still close.

Kim was in the county seat for eight years before deciding to run for mayor.

"I was very political. I mean, I'm still political but not as active as I was. I was kind of a mental case," she says, laughing. "I ran for mayor because I felt like the city needed somebody . . . I hate to say 'somebody like me,' but they needed someone energetic, who could be a leader, who would do something, and who wasn't afraid to take risks. The mayor at the time was a good mayor, but he didn't do things unless he knew the outcome was going to be positive. Whereas, I was always like, 'Let's do this.' I was in a position to do stuff. I had a really good network at the state and federal government, so I knew I could access resources, which we did," she says.

Where we are sitting is one of the big things Kim did during her time as mayor. Muller Plaza used to be a big empty lot in the middle of Oneonta's Main Street. The original buildings there had been knocked down during an urban renewal project in the 1970s, yet nothing had been built.

With a downtown rebound plan as part of her campaign, Kim promised that a hotel would be built on the lot within two years. She accomplished this by learning the city code and being willing to play a little good cop/bad cop with the lot's owner, a developer in Ithaca, two hours away. Whenever the property was out of compliance with city policy on trash removal, the code officer would fine the absentee owner, whom Kim started to "schmooze" in order to get him to the negotiating table. Eventually, the city had a Clarion hotel on the lot, which promptly became fully booked for college activities such as sporting events, Parents' Weekend, and graduations. The city also boasted a public space for parades, protests, holiday celebrations, and a weekly farmers' market.

After two terms, Kim stepped down for two reasons. Her personal relationship was breaking up, she says, which caused her to lose her confidence. Also, she needed to have a full-time income because she was now a single parent.

"I was just in a place where I didn't believe in myself, and that was really hard," she says. "I've thought about that decision a lot. You always do the best you can at the time, but it kind of made me mad that I didn't do it again. I mean, there was all this cool stuff that would have happened. On the other hand . . ." Her voice trails off.

"Do you ever think about going back?" I ask.

"No," she says. "I mean, do I ever think about it? Yes. I always said I'd love to run against state senator Jim Seward, just to beat him. I don't want his job. I just want to beat him. I love doing campaigns."

"I'm the exact opposite," I say. "I don't want to do a campaign. Just give me the job, and I'll do that."

"There are things I don't like about campaigning, but the challenge, I love," she says.

"What didn't you like about campaigning?"

"The door-to-door. I used to fake door-to-door. It sounds terrible. I mean, my first year I did door-to-door. Once I got elected, I would do, like, one block in all different parts of the city," she says.

Kim is a big believer in local politics and remains involved in it. It's important, she says, "because you're living in the middle of it. It's the place where we can really make a direct impact that is seen. It still takes negotiation with other people, but it's easier to make a difference."

Her belief in women getting into local politics is twice as large as her love for the local system itself. "Women are the best to lean into the heart and souls of their communities," she says. "I don't want to stereotype too much, but I'm willing to stereotype a fair amount. Women are connected in the communities and their organizations. They tend to be more active in the schools with their children, so I think they just have a better sense of what's going on. And they work differently and are able to work in cooperative ways where they're not threatened and are able to change their minds. You don't have this, 'Oh my God, you're challenging my authority.' I used to make decisions all the time as mayor. I'd have department meetings and say, 'Do this and this.' They almost never did what I decided, but what I decided was a catalyst for them doing *something*. Do something—even if it's just to show me that I'm wrong."

◌ ◌ ◌

The something *I* was doing now was wandering the neighborhood again with my clipboard, looking for registered Democrats who were (a) home and (b) able to sign. The whole process struck me as old-fashioned, given that we were living in the internet age. Heck, the Russians weaponized social media to influence a presidential election. I ought to be able to use it on a much smaller scale to avoid the tedium of getting voters to sign a form. There ought to be an app for this. (I later learned that there *is* an app for "cutting turf," the term of art for figuring out which doors to knock on. In my frantic scramble to get to Election Day with my sanity reasonably intact, I hadn't researched apps, and I found out about this one only because the *Pod Save America* guys mentioned it. Yet the cost of the app was prohibitive for such a small campaign.)

As I've said, getting your name on the ballot for the party you are registered in is a matter of collecting the correct number of signatures. It's a little trickier when you want to run on another party's line. If I wasn't a registered Democrat, I would join the Working Families Party, which has a relatively robust (for a third party) presence in New York. In order to bogart their imprimatur while still running as a Democrat, I had to fill out a form, pass a phone interview, and get one party member of the four in the district to sign a separate petition.

I love a good form, so that was easy enough. I can tolerate a phone interview, so that was fine. I knew a couple of Working

Families Party people, so it seemed like that would be a snap, too.

There was a trick to it, though.

The one signature I needed had to be collected by either another party member or by me and notarized at the time of signing. Any way I looked at it, I needed two other people to meet me somewhere at the same time: either two Working Families folk or one of them and a notary. After far more phone calls and text messages than any reasonable person would expect to make, I met up in a church parking lot with a member of the Hill City Rollers roller derby team (the Working Families party member) and said church's organist (the notary). Sunday mornings can be weird.

I knew both of them through a now-defunct knitting group. The only time we could find when all three of us were available was the ten-minute break before the church service started. I'd just finished a long run, hadn't showered yet, and was dripping sweat onto the petition, which was signed and notarized on the tailgate of my ancient Kia Sportage. Worshippers were filing into the church as the three of us dispersed to our regular Sunday routines.

The signature collecting seems simultaneously too cumbersome and too simple, somehow. All the paper forms, with their very specific requirements, that have to be hand-carried around a neighborhood and collated in an intricately delineated manner are like something from the horse-and-buggy era. As far as I was concerned, all this dead tree rigamarole should have been left back with the Lindy Hop.

Yet, it also felt too easy to get on a ballot. The only test was my ability to walk around a couple dozen blocks and knock on doors? Or, if I couldn't walk it personally, the hoop I had to jump through would have been knowing enough trustworthy people to act as my agents. That's it? There was no licensing body or written exam or credit check? I'm just spitballing here, but this might be why we're in our current predicament. Of course, instituting tests and credit checks would lead to all manner of discrimination, which makes me think that this low bar to entry is a feature rather than a bug.

Simply getting your name on a ballot isn't the same as running a campaign. The shoe leather parts are good practice for meeting those who live closest to you, mind, but they're still a far cry from convincing them that you know what you're doing. And it's doubly hard to convince them that you know what you're doing when you actually have no idea what you're doing.

I'm a terrible actress, even though my first degree is in theater. I was on the tech side, though, not the performance side. If you need lights hung or a flat painted, I'm your huckleberry. Look elsewhere for soaring oratory delivered convincingly.

Most of what I gleaned about campaigns and issues came from podcasts such as *Pod Save America*. The voices of Jon Favreau, Tommy Vietor, Dan Pfeiffer, and Jon Lovett, four (comparatively) young dudes who worked for Obama, kept me fired up and sane amid weeks of *Washington Post* push notices and Twitter-induced outrage fatigue.

Former speechwriter Favreau made it clear that the first two questions a candidate should be able to answer are "why me?" and "why now?" And while I walked around my district collecting signatures after work—which meant that I caught voters mostly when they were in the middle of making dinner and wrangling hungry children, and were therefore disinclined to talk much—I noodled around with my answers. About the best answers I came up with were "Somebody has to, and I am somebody" and, for the second question, a vague interpretive dance that included gestures to everything around me and imparted a sense of chaos and loss.

Even two years later, I'm not sure I've improved on my core belief: civilization doesn't happen unless we all pitch in. I've added a small codicil after my time in office. When it all seems futile and overwhelming, boil it down to a simple question: "Am I making life for a random stranger worse or better?" Decisions and policy are easier when you add that frame of reference.

CHAPTER 7

Local Campaign? Local Issues

Once I got beyond defining my campaign's broad organizing principles, I had to figure out what I saw for Otsego County. This would have been a snap if I had already known what the particular problems were in said county. We have the same basic hot buttons that every community faces. We need more good jobs, clean energy, and affordable housing. We need less crime, less opioid use, and fewer people reliant on food banks. So does everyone else.

Local campaigns need to focus on local issues, if only because they can. You can say, specifically, that the intersection of Routes 101 and 9 is dangerous and you're going to fix it. It's probably an intersection everyone knows. That's harder to do on a larger scale. Saying that North Korea should denuclearize is swell, but most voters aren't going to have firsthand knowledge of North Korea or nukes.

When I started to dig into it, I saw that some of the issues in my county were the same faced by most rural counties. A big one was the availability of reliable high-speed internet access. It's not a problem that I personally face. I live in the city, and there are two colleges here. The population is dense—

not in terms of its ability to absorb information (although this could be up for debate), but because many of us live within a stone's throw of one another—and its students' demands drive our tech infrastructure. But once you get a couple of minutes outside the city, not even Dwayne "The Rock" Johnson could throw a, um, rock and hit his nearest neighbor. The vast cable conglomerates aren't doing a bang-up job of moving into these areas, and even a humanities major like me can understand why.

Compare broadband infrastructure to a network of roads. You build multilane highways around, through, and over the parts where all the people live, and each of those people pays a little bit of tax money to build the big roads. That small individual investment gives those city folk a zippy way to access the wider world.

The rural dwellers want to be part of the wider world, too, and not just as tourist attractions for the city people who "want to get away from it all" and "see how the simple folk live." They want to be able to buy exotic coffees and experience the ballet and sell their artisanal mustache wax, too. But it's just so time-consuming to access the wider world when the road to it is little more than a narrow, winding dirt path that washes out whenever it rains.

The big road builders, however, have zero interest in paving those rural roads because the return on investment is so low. Interstate highways are expensive to build. And when the builders look at how many miles of road you'd need to connect all those far-flung houses and at how much you'd have to charge each house just to recoup the cost, they conclude that it's just not worth it. Besides, the people living out there aren't swimming in dough, so why bother trying to bring them into the larger economy?

This is the kind of problem governments can solve. After

all, private industry didn't build roads into rural areas out of the goodness of its heart. The community decided it was important for all its members to move around with relative ease, and told their representatives to make it happen, even if it meant taxpayers would need to chip in an extra dime or two. In short, building roads (or a power grid or canals or railroads) is a public good.

Broadband is the interstate system of the early twenty-first century. Rural residents need it for education, business, and communication. No one will settle in an area without it. But until someone figures out a way to get the internet everywhere without having to run fiber optic lines underground or over-head, the cost to get it to isolated areas will always be greater than any return realized per customer. The machinery of gov-ernment could make it happen, if the voters want it to.

In New York, they've made it clear that they do. Even so, making it happen has been the hard part. A couple of years ago, when Time Warner Cable was gobbling up smaller companies, one of the deals it made with state regulators was that it would reach into rural communities in exchange for the state letting it become one ginormous glob of telecommunications services. And because we learned nothing from playing Monopoly as kids, the State of New York signed off on this.

In hindsight, what the state should have done is flip the game board, scattering all the candy-colored cash and the tokens and hotels around the living room, because the big cable companies snuck hundred-dollar bills out of the bank whenever the state went to the bathroom. But here we are.

The glob of telecommunications services I mentioned is now called Spectrum and has done more or less nothing over the past few years to make good on its promise to be an upstanding corporate citizen. Currently, there's litigation pending on the state level, which is nice and all, but the original problem still remains: rural areas don't have broadband.

While the day may come when the state and Spectrum come to an agreement, local government shouldn't hold its breath. There are other ways to get the work done, as it turns out, if we can figure out how to move the money where it needs to be.

All that is what I should have said when I was confronted by a local business leader at a Democratic fund-raiser held at a local brew pub. The event was hosted by a local environmental protection group that had had good luck supporting candidates opposed to fracking.

Otsego sits on top of the Marcellus Shale, the same geologic formation that has been exploited in Central Pennsylvania. Our economic conditions are the same, too. Lots of New York farmers sold the right to drill on their land to lots of gas companies, and that income kept them afloat in rough financial seas. Those initial leases are drying up, however, because fracking isn't going to happen here.

The fracking boom made our southern neighbor lots of money, but it has also cost a lot of money. Gas trucks tear up the roads, which require constant widening and repaving. The trucks themselves aren't super safe, given that they are filled with compressed gas that can potentially explode in an accident. No one is 100 percent certain that fracking chemicals aren't going to do long-lasting harm to the environment, and research suggests that removing that much gas from the earth's crust is making it unstable. Indeed, there was a rogue earthquake in the area a few years back that felt like a not-so-subtle reminder that our houses are built on marginally stable layers of rock and gas and water. (In case it's not abundantly clear, I think fracking is a bad idea. Just wanted to get that on the record.)

So far, this environmental protection group (and others like it statewide) has blocked natural gas extraction in New York State. Its success has given it a lot of pull on the local political scene, hence its hosting this fund-raiser to further the cause. The bar where it was held was part brewery, part Indian restaurant, one of those delightfully quirky places that can thrive in a small city.

Shortly after each candidate made introductory remarks to the crowd, the leader of the Otsego County Chamber of Commerce—her kids and mine attended the same day care back in the day, and we're friendly but not friends, if that makes sense—asked for my thoughts about broadband access. Instead of giving her that cogent argument about how important it was because we can improve outcomes only if everyone can unleash the power of the internet, I stammered something about how it wasn't my biggest concern because I, personally, had great internet service in my district.

Pro tip: this is the wrong answer. I could tell by how quickly this woman closed the conversation and walked away.

For the record, I was drinking water, not beer. (I'm not a huge drinker, mostly because I get red-cheeked and super sleepy when I drink. Besides, I'd rather save my booze calories for dessert.) And in my defense, this took place only a week or two into my official campaign, when I was standing in front of a firehose of information holding nothing but a cocktail umbrella to keep myself dry. The only way I could start to make sense of all I was learning was to focus on what would most affect the eight-hundred-plus people in my district. They were the ones I needed to get out of their houses and into the polling place. Once that happened, I could figure out the rest on the fly.

I have a tendency to freeze up when asked an easy question I know has a complicated answer that the asker may not want to sit through. I'm the one you want for a witty quip to break the tension. Meaty-but-brisk soundbites aren't in my wheelhouse. What I should have said was, "Otsego Countians can't be part of the twenty-first century without equal access to its tools. Getting that equal access is a heavy lift, but one we can manage with the right leverage."

See? So much more satisfying, and it has the added advantage of being true.

◦ ◦ ◦

At the same time that I was learning how to talk about the problems my community faced, I was also figuring out how to fund yard signs, flyers, and newspaper ads. While I was willing to pony up the money myself, I thought I'd ask for some from other people first—such as small groups of environmentalists in a local bar, or the county Democratic Party, whose website read more like that for a social club than for a vibrant political organization. This is an observation rather than a mean-spirited dig. In a largely Republican county, Democrats need all the moral support they can get. And from an organizing perspective, progressives took too much for granted during the Obama years. We got lazy.

I had no idea what to expect when I went to the Democratic Party's "Candidate Night," when every potential Dem in the race sits for questions from the party's organizing members. The event was held at the party president's house, in one of the nicer parts of Cooperstown—its nice parts rival the smaller towns on Cape Cod—near the Otesaga Hotel. The Otesaga is where most of the Baseball Hall of Fame inductees stay, and is on the National Register of Historic Places. Syfy's *Ghost Hunters* filmed an episode there, because anything built in 1909 *must* be haunted.

During the start of the meeting that evening, we candidates

waited in the kitchen, introducing ourselves to one another and eating cookies. The party's goal in 2017 was to have someone run for every potential office, and it had done a great job of shaking the bushes until enough able bodies fell out, a few of whom I got to know fairly well during the course of the campaign. Cathy K. was running in nearby Otego for the seat currently held by another Kathy (Kathy C.), the entrenched county board chair. Later I'd meet Danny, a native Californian with a passion for public planning who'd gotten his degree from nearby Bard College; he was running in one of the city districts.

Soon, one by one, we were called over to the hot seat, which was a stool in the living room that we could see from the kitchen. My time as interviewee was a cross between being in the witness box in court and on a dating show. Yes, I told the party members, I do support left-leaning ideas such as equal pay and sustainable clean energy and health care as a human right. Love is, in fact, love, and no, we shouldn't destroy the environment we live in.

That was more or less it for the questions. While I did briefly wonder if I was going to be asked to show my teeth to those assembled, the interview was straightforward if awkward, and less about my bona fides than about my ability to speak in complete sentences—until we got to money, which was the reason we were all there in the first place.

It's ideal to have your party's spiritual buy-in, but it's even better to have its cold, hard cash. The party chair asked about this directly: will you put your own money in?

"Yes," I said. What I thought (but didn't say) was "Will you?"

This is going to come as a huge shock—you might want to sit down—but women tend to have problems when it comes to talking about money. Don't get me wrong. We can talk about money when we're asked to define it or speculate as to how much something costs. What we suck at is demanding it in exchange for our time, experience, and effort.

This hesitation feeds into the income gender gap, which is the whole "white women earn eighty-two cents for every dollar a man earns." While a big old base of overt gender discrimination supports that statistic, so does the subtle conditioning of living in a world where men are at the top of the power structure. It's hard to ask for more money when you've been told you don't deserve it or when you lack the training to know how to ask. (Yes, this is changing. Yes, not all men. Yes, J. K. Rowling makes bricks of cash. But I'm talking about the system at large.)

I'm terrible at asking for money, epically so. Early in my writing career, I balked at sending invoices for payments that had already been agreed on. It took me years to stop working for free, even if my payment was something as nontransferable as a T-shirt or loaves of homemade bread. I still approach writing that way, but I now have an agent for larger projects who talks me out of my own worst financial impulses.

Still, you can't run for office without asking for money. It's what keeps the whole body lurching forward, and it's a good way to measure support and voter buy-in. And one of the many upsides of running for a local office is that it doesn't take that much money to make it happen.

I understood only bits of this until the local Dems held a workshop with Leslie Danks Burke and Denise King, the women behind Trailblazers, a political action committee based in the Finger Lakes. Their four-hour presentation on the concept of "front porch politics" helped me stop flailing (as much) and develop a plan. Of the two, Leslie is the more dynamic speaker, a skill she likely honed during her recent run for state office. Denise is more measured, but her words have the weight of authority. As much as I hate the word *transformative*, their workshop really was. I walked out of there with clarity and a renewed mission, and I have kept up with Leslie and Denise since I met them because they truly know their shit.

The Trailblazers PAC started in 2017 after Leslie lost her bid for a New York State Senate seat the year before. Denise, Leslie's campaign manager, was a founding member of Eleanor's Legacy, a national PAC that supports pro-choice candidates, and had been cochair for Howard Dean's 2004 presidential campaign and senior adviser to Kristen Gillibrand's 2006 congressional race. After Leslie lost, both women and their deputy campaign manager, Joe Messmer, looked at the voter data.

"We realized that even though we lost, something really different had happened in our campaign," Leslie says. "If you look at the numbers, there are thirty-two percent Democrats in the district, and we ended up getting forty-five percent of the vote in 2016, which was not a really good year for Democrats, right?"

After discovering this, the three started combing through data from other districts for races that skewed by 13 percent over the base registration, and they found none.

"So, whatever we had done in the Fifty-eighth Senate District in New York State against a sitting Republican incumbent was really different from what candidates were doing on either side of the aisle," Leslie says.

Their post mortem revealed two things that they had done differently from other campaigns in the state. First, they raised money from outside traditional fundraising circles such as PACs and the large real estate lobbies. Yes, Leslie says, real estate interests have deep pockets and are bipartisan, but they are also transactional. They tend to give to incumbents, not upstarts, because incumbents are in a position to support their interests.

Leslie's campaign didn't have a moral reason for avoiding these traditional avenues for cash; it just wasn't in a position to take advantage of them. "I was running in a district that was skewed dramatically against my political party, and so they just weren't interested," Leslie says. "So we had to find money from somewhere else. We ended up outraising my opponent, and also outraising every other state senate challenger in the state. How? We raised money from inside the district."

At the final tally, they found that 85 percent of the donations to Leslie's campaign came from the five-county area comprising the state senate district she ran in. Her opponent raised 65 percent of his funds from zip codes in Albany, the state capital, and New York City, neither of which is near the district.

"Our view is that it's not just about small-dollar donations. It's about voter dollars. It's about [the] people who actually can vote for the candidate having a financial stake in the campaign, [of their] actually being bought in, literally invest[ing] in the campaign," Leslie says.

The first thing that was different was whom the money came from. The second was that her campaign disclosed 100 percent of income and expenditures. The campaign made this choice not to climb onto an ethical high horse, but because it was easier to do it that way.

"I'm a lawyer," Leslie says. "I have my professional career. I have my job taking care of my kids and my household as a mom. Then I had my political career. I didn't have time to become an expert on election law. So, I looked at this as a lawyer and I said the easiest way to never break the law in this is just to overdisclose. Disclose everything. So we did."

Near as the trio could tell, these were the two factors that skewed the numbers in their favor, even though Leslie lost. But rather than pack up their leftover campaign funds and call it a day, they founded Trailblazers. The PAC's focus is "front porch politics," which brings the campaign to the voters, asks for their support, and shows them what that support has done.

"Our theory at the beginning . . . is that if you're more honest and open and you engage your voters and your campaign through fundraising, you're more likely to win. It turns out to be a theory that's true. Over half of the candidates that we invest in end up winning their races. Isn't that wonderful? That being a more honest person also makes you a more powerful candidate," Leslie says.

Since its founding, Trailblazers has grown from Leslie, Denise, and Joe into a full-fledged operation with more than twenty stakeholders and a new office, which it had to move to when the old office got too small. At first, the PAC focused its energy on candidates in New York and Pennsylvania. Now it is expanding nationwide, with candidates in Chicago and Missouri and workshops planned all over the place.

I went into that workshop with Leslie and Denise as nervous as an Australian Shepherd with disorganized sheep; I left with a solid plan on what I needed to do next. On that list was to ask more potential voters to give me money, mostly so that I could then ask Trailblazers to do the same, as before it will consider endorsing you, a percentage of the dollars in your kitty needs to have come from your district.

This meant working through my fear of talking about the green stuff.

Leslie brings this up in the workshops. Generally, if there are more women in the room than men, "I will talk to the women and say, 'Look, we gotta recognize that since birth, we have been told not to ask for things. That's just part of being female in America.' So, when you're going out there to ask for donations or for votes or for media attention—whatever it is you're trying to get in your campaign—you have to overcome this internal sensor that is telling you not to ask for anything.

"That's hard," she says. "Women have that additional challenge they're facing when they're asking for donations—and a way to think about the money is to take it off its pedestal and recognize that it's just dollars. If you can go out there and ask for someone's vote, that's priceless. You're asking a person for their faith in you as a leader. That's a pretty big ask. If you can have the guts to ask someone for their vote, then, goodness gracious, you can ask them for money. What you're really doing is asking for [their] faith in you as a leader, and what you're asking is permission to be the person who carries the voice forward."

The "asking permission" part is tough for most women to do. Our conditioning to be happy with what we're given and not to demand more is deeply ingrained in us and so very hard to work through. Actually, working through it is too big a challenge. The best we can do might be to acknowledge that it exists and try to be a little bit better at asking every day. The rewards can be great, especially if you'd like to make a difference in your community.

The majority of candidates Trailblazers supports are women running for local offices. Trailblazers has made the choice to support only those campaigning for county-level office or below, because these are the positions that go unnoticed by bigger organizations, have more impact on daily life in any community, and incur smaller costs. (Less than two thousand dollars can swing a race.)

"Whether it's school board or village trustee or town board or county legislature, it's closest to home, and women are jumping in at all levels. We know that now, post 2016," Denise says. "But prior to that, it was the place [for] a woman who wanted to do public service and still be able to do her other jobs in the home and also in work. Politics usually becomes a third career for women. The place that they feel like they can contribute the most is at the local level. That's been proven over time."

And once in local office, women's reelection rate is higher than that of their male counterparts. Denise has a theory as to why this is so: "It's because they listen. They pick their battles and they figure out those things that can get done. Because that's how we balance our lives. All of those things that we learn to manage, whether it's money, people's time, schedules, setting priorities—we're just used to it. That's why when we get elected, it's a very logical leap from PTA president to village mayor," she says.

"I wish that there were some little magic elixir that we could give to people that would make them understand that these things are important," she says. "I had this candidate. She was running on sewers, sidewalks, and public safety. That's really what mattered to the people. She did get elected, by the way, and is going to be a great mayor."

"Money is such a bigger problem at the local level," Leslie adds, "and nobody thinks about it. Just imagine if somebody came in and found some not very well-meaning person that wanted to write a check for a really small amount of money. You could swing a whole board."

It's more common than many voters realize, the dark money Leslie alludes to. While dark money—that is, donations from sources the public can't see—plays a huge role in our national elections, it floods into local races, too. You can buy a whole county board for less than one state senator, and the result can have a more immediate bearing on, say, a zoning variance your firm needs.

It's a sobering thought. Local governments, which have more power over everything from housing the homeless to maintaining safe drinking water, are easy prey for anyone with a few thousand dollars and an agenda. Why look nationally if you really want to make a change you can see?

"In our own area, large organizations came in and got involved in local elections because they wanted to keep the people that were in power in power, for their own benefit," Leslie says. "There is dark money in local politics. Nobody pays attention to it."

The focus on local offices gives Leslie and Denise a sense of well-being because even if the national political agenda seems to be fascist-curious, some parts of the country will hold the line.

"Knowing that in all of these little communities, all over the two states that we work in and, now that we're going national, all over the country, in each one of those little communities, it's gonna be okay," Leslie says. "To know that we have these forty candidates that we've worked with in forty different municipalities—each one of those individual people are taking this message of government belonging to the voters and how important local politics is. That feels really good. That's what I'm most proud of: the multiplier effect of all these individuals changing their small worlds."

CHAPTER 8

Calculate Your Win Number

The Trailblazer workshop wasn't all pep talk. I came out of it with a plan.

Actually, not a plan per se, but a plan of what I needed to figure out to start to have a plan, which was a substantial improvement over what I had before the workshop, which was nausea and a sense that I should be doing more.

Some of Leslie and Denise's suggestions weren't feasible for me. They'd stressed that the candidate should be the face of the campaign, the one who gets the message across to voters, and at bare minimum, there should be a separate person as campaign manager, the one who takes care of logistics, the checkbook, and messaging. In a perfect world, four other people would be taking care of field organization, social media, a database, and fundraising, working in tandem with the manager. But at this point—the election was only four months away—I felt that the district was small enough that I didn't need to drag in more people.

I may not have had all the bodies, but I could still assemble a strategy to make best use of the resources I had, and that required first calculating what we call my "win number."

A win number is fairly self-explanatory. You need 50 percent of the votes plus one vote to win. If you're a suspenders-and-belt type, shoot for 52 percent of the votes, to give yourself enough of a cushion in case of a recount and/or hanging chads. Fortunately, all the numbers you need to calculate this are public information on file with your county board of elections.

Step one: Find the data for the last couple of times your intended office was contested. Our county elections are always in odd years; for me that was 2015 and 2013. It can get tricky if your office is contested in the even years, because every four years you will run into the presidential election, which inflates the numbers in less predictable ways. Regardless, even presidential year info will get you in the ballpark.

Here are the numbers I needed to know:

- There are 880-ish voters in the district.
- In 2015, 315 of them voted, 180 for the incumbent and 135 for the challenger.
- In 2013, 281 of them voted, 144 for the incumbent and 137 for the challenger.

Assuming that the higher number was more likely in 2017, 50 percent + 1 of 316 (because you can't have fractional votes) is 159. To err on the side of caution, let's say my win number was 164—granted, a ridiculously small number of people for a countywide office.

$\circ$ $\circ$ $\circ$

Once you know that win number, you can calculate how you think you might get there based on party registration. This information is also available from the Board of Elections, which will even email it to you in a searchable .csv file, which should make every numbers nerd giddy.

In 2017, of the registered voters:

- 181 had no party affiliation.
- 22 were from the Green, Conservative, Libertarian, or Working Families Party.
- 43 were from the Independence Party (not Independent Party, but a percentage of them probably thought they were).
- 174 were Republican.
- 457 were Democrats.

These statistics make it seem that this should be an easy win for the Democratic candidate, and in past years, it was. In 2009, Catherine Rothenberger, the Dem, received 261 votes, while Craig Gelbsman, the Republican incumbent I was running against in 2017, received 153. In 2011, the final count was Rothenberger's 220 to Gelbsman's 50.

Hmm. So, why the switch to Republican?

My conclusion? Even though the district had gone Republican for the last four years, there was no good reason that it should now. The Democratic candidate in 2013 and 2015 is a lovely person who failed to connect with voters. They didn't so much vote against her as not vote at all.

Next, I needed to figure out what to do to get to my magic number of 164. My approach was to divide the district up into three pools of voters: base, persuadables, and never-gonna-happen-ers. Base voters, who can figure out what you are about because of your party membership, generally just need to be reminded that an election is coming up, where the polling place is, and why it is so very important that they get off their fannies at some point that day and cast a ballot. The Dems in my district weren't covering themselves in glory with regard to that last point. Fewer than half of them could be bothered.

I mean, come on! It's the least you can do if you give anything resembling a shit. I know, I know. Lecturing people never works, but seriously now.

And I refuse to believe the "I couldn't make the time" excuse, at least not in Oneonta. Our polls open at 6 a.m. and stay open until 9 p.m., which gives voters a full fifteen hours to get there. The location itself has ample parking, is on a bus route, and is handicap accessible. I have never waited more than five minutes to cast my vote, even right after work, when the place is busy. In short, it's Not. That. Hard.

Granted, my little town isn't the country at large, where there are huge problems: endless lines, polling places that are hard to find or are open for limited hours, to say nothing of flat-out voter suppression. But the place where I live isn't one of those. You even get a sticker. Sometimes, there are cookies. I'm not sure how much more user-friendly it could be.

To sum up: what I needed to do with the base (that is, voters already on the left-hand side) was remind them to do their part.

The next group, the voters who could be persuaded, included those who hadn't checked a box for party preference when they registered to vote. All those folks needed was persuasion, plus a reminder to vote.

The third group comprised my opponent's base, which would be the registered Republicans, Independence Party people, and Libertarians. The odds of their being persuadable were low, with one exception. A small slice of Republican women might be tired of the macho excess of the national party and be willing to listen to a message from the other side. If I had extra time after I'd worked on the first two groups, I'd take a swing at this wedge of the electorate.

For those of you who've watched *Mad Men*, you might have noticed that this audience segmentation resembles that for an advertising campaign, and it is. Advertisers must first figure out what the given product is used for and then plot how to reach the target consumer as much as possible and in as many different ways as they can. Only instead of selling a fresh twist on toilet paper or a wireless service I was selling myself, which is weird.

Conveniently, my day job in SUNY Oneonta's alumni office was marketing adjacent. In the organizational chart of my division of the college, my little alumni magazine editor box is connected to a larger-than-you-think network of professionals whose job it is to persuade people to donate to the school. Our mission is to demonstrate how those dollars are used to help students get an education just like the one that an alumnus or alumna has found valuable.

The remaining disaffected Gen-X sliver of my soul is appalled that a multimillion-dollar entity asks for donations from people who already dropped a lot of cash just to get their degrees. The rest of me has seen the balance sheets and knows how much it takes to deliver a quality education at a reasonable price, especially during a time when education is the first to be cut when state revenue gets tight.

I believe that little SUNY O does a great job of teaching students how to think and preparing them for whatever they choose to do next. That belief in the product's value makes it an easy sell. It's harder when that product is yourself.

What I do believe in, however, is focusing on the task at hand rather than on my decades-long case of imposter syndrome. That's right. I will go to my deathbed convinced that there is somebody out there worthier than I am of doing whatever it is I'm doing. I shouldn't run a marathon, or have a baby, or have another baby, or write a book, because I know deep, deep down that someone will notice that I don't know what I'm doing. Someone will figure out how much I am winging it and will point and laugh, because everyone else clearly has it all under control, which I know isn't true but can't quite accept.

But those people who do know exactly how to do it aren't stepping up to do it. Somebody has to. It might as well be me.

CHAPTER 9

"It's Complicated!" Is Not Messaging

Once I'd sorted out the groups of people likely to vote for me, I needed to figure out how to get my message to them. And once I figured out the how, I could finally focus on what that message might be. I couldn't run on my vast political experience, because I had none. I couldn't run on my deep understanding of the issues facing the county, because my understanding of them was shallow at best and not likely to become any more than ankle-deep before the election. Counties do so much to make civilized life possible that it would take a decade for me to understand how it all interlocked. And I had only a couple of months.

Pro tip: "It's complicated" is not a winning message.

As I've mentioned, I put the message part on the back burner and, with apologies to Marshall McLuhan, turned my attention to the medium. And the media at my disposal were postcards and other mailables, ads in the newspaper and on Facebook, and my voice through the air when I spoke to voters. See? I paid attention during my Communications Theory class.

In larger areas, mass media such as TV and the radio

should be in the mix. Here, however, most of the local stations come from cities at least an hour away, with enormous coverage. Ninety-nine percent of the people who saw an ad for me wouldn't be in my district, which meant the return on investment would be frighteningly low. Besides, buying a TV spot required much more money than I had. Ditto radio, which I'm not even convinced people listen to anymore, now that we have phones and podcasts and Sirius XM.

The idea was to touch every voter a couple of times. I'm using the marketing definition of *touch*, which means reminding an individual that you exist, rather than the definition that earns you a visit from HR. My goal was to have three good touches (rim shot) on every friendly voter.

The internet has made designing "collateral material" (i.e., flyers and postcards) so much easier than it was in the olden days, when we had to hand-crank them out on the letterpress machine by candlelight after walking uphill both ways in the snow. Every online printer has a template for just about every imaginable document your little political heart could desire. Need a yard sign? Done. Need a trifold flyer? Sure. In the market for a manifesto made from letters cut out of magazines about how your opponent is a tool of the Illuminati? Overnight shipping will cost extra.

I'd been advised to use a family picture, ideally one with my dog in the frame, too. My oldest kid had just started high school, and the youngest was in his first year of middle school—two hard transitions as it was. So, for all my ambition, I just couldn't slap my kids' faces on something that would wind up in all their friends' mailboxes at this critical juncture in their lives.

My husband was game, but a photo of just the two of us seemed weird—"She talks about having children, but no one has ever seen them" weird. Are they allergic to the sun? Is this a *Who's Afraid of Virginia Woolf* situation? So, I art-directed my spouse out of the photo.

I was tempted to take a picture with my dog—being a corgi, she is super cute and a complete diva—but I couldn't afford the ten grand it would have taken just to get her out of bed, much less the snacks on her talent rider. This brought it down to a photo of me by my lonesome.

To be honest, the picture I slapped on every single handout might have been what won the election for me. It's a head shot a friend from college took a couple of years ago. Somehow, after careful application of lipstick and eyeliner, her mad shooting skills transformed my standard exhausted librarian look into that of an approachable, responsible adult. No one was more shocked than I.

The postcards were simple to assemble. My face plus my name plus district info on the front; a reminder about when the election was on the back, with plenty of white space where I could write a personal note. Go to the online printer of your choice, pick one of the predesigned templates under the "election" theme—they come in every combination of colors as long as those colors are red, white, and blue—plug it all in, and boom! Done. Once I had them in hand, the postcards went out mostly as thank-you notes to people who were donating money or time. Because nothing conveys gratitude like a picture of your face.

The mailer was harder to put together because it required actual words. I knocked out the easy parts first: picture, district info, name, election date and place reminder. Thanks to the workshop with Denise and Leslie, and after I filled out a few forms, I'd won an endorsement from Trailblazers. I had also notched one from Sustainable Otsego, a local PAC that promotes green practices in the region, and from Eleanor's Legacy. Gary Herzig, Oneonta's current mayor, and Kim Muller, its former mayor, both wrote endorsements. While I'd like to say it was an arduous process to secure them, I really just politely asked.

For the harder section of the mailer, I wrote a paragraph owning up to my not having grown up in Otsego County, as my opponent had, which I had been told could be an issue. My focus was on my having *chosen* to live here and the fact that, fifteen years later, I had zero intention of ever leaving. Even my dad, who had lived in Ohio for the last couple of decades, had moved here when he retired. We hadn't intended for him to live across the street from us, but weirdly, it has worked out, and it's only a matter of time before there is a whole Martini compound on Cedar Street. Why would I leave that behind?

All this was not enough to fill a mailer, however. What I needed to do was articulate why I was a good choice for the county board. Oddly enough, Al Franken's voice is what caused my message to crystalize.

I know I'm wading into some marshy territory here, but this happened long before Franken's behavior got him booted from the Senate. While I have an opinion—short version: he did a lot of good work but shouldn't have grabbed women without their consent—I'm not willing to retroactively pretend he wasn't an influence on how I came to understand the point of government. Your mileage, of course, may vary.

I figured it out on a family road trip. The four of us—kids, husband, and I—were listening to Franken's *Giant of the Senate* in the car. (Yes, our young nerd apples didn't fall far from the nerd trees. Mostly, I suspect they listened along because Franken's funny and sometimes swears. When they got bored, they went back to playing on any number of electronic devices they had within arm's reach, as true computer natives do.) Franken kicks off *Giant* with an anecdote about his wife's mother, Franni, who grew up dirt poor but rose to the middle class through hard work and a boost from government programs such as the GI Bill, Pell Grants, and Social Security. "They tell you in this country that you have to pull yourself up by your bootstraps. And we all believe that. But first you've got to have the boots. And the federal government gave Franni's family the boots," Franken writes.

Franken goes on to talk about his idol/mentor Paul Wellstone, a U.S. senator from Minnesota who was killed in a plane crash in 2002. One of Wellstone's catchphrases was "We all do better when we all do better," which is both fun to type and fundamentally true. Our communities don't function well when a percentage of the people comprising them don't even have boots.

One of the main purposes of government is to ensure equal boot ownership. It's up to the individual to pull him- or herself up after that—which isn't the same as wanting to redistribute boots so that everyone has exactly the same number of them. If you are a boot baron, great! Keep 'em. It's just that if you don't have any boots, society as a whole should spend a few bucks to get you a pair. It's a self-interested act of charity. Your contributions to the social good through labor or ideas or care will pay the collective us back.

That boot metaphor is what I saw for Otsego County. In recent years, the loudest voices on the county board had seemed unable or unwilling to admit that resisting every new idea presented to them wasn't helping anyone do better. You can't grow productive citizens by cutting back on air, sunlight, and water. True, there were lean years after the financial crisis in 2008, when some hard choices had to be made. Still, as long as there was a financial cushion "just in case," I felt we shouldn't cut budgets to the bone merely out of principle. If we could figure out how to get more boots to more people, we could increase the county's productivity.

But before the county could come up with new ways of looking at old problems, it had to break up the Republican majority that had no incentive to listen to the other side—which is why it was time to elect a fresh face, someone who wanted us all to do better by investing our energy in protecting our resources, both human and environmental, and by ensuring equal access to decent health care, quality education, and jobs that paid a living wage.

If you are going to dream, dream big.

○ ○ ○

In addition to my soaring Paul Wellstone testimony about boots and straps and doing better, I had a couple of specific action items that would make our county government more responsive to the needs of the people who actually lived there, as opposed to the needs of the people currently on the board. In a perfect world, the county would have reasonable meeting times and an elected county manager.

Regarding the former, most county business is done during banker's hours. The main board meetings, which are held on the first Wednesday of the month, last from 10 a.m. until whenever they are done. If you are an adult with a job who also wants to be see how Otsego makes its legislation, you have to take the day off. Convening the meeting, or at least the parts of the meeting that could be controversial, at a time when more people can come would be the right thing to do.

Taking a day off isn't a big deal if you own your own business or are retired, which described more than half the sitting board members at the time. It also isn't a big deal if you work someplace, as I do, where taking time off requires nothing more than asking for it. But such hours make it impossible for hourly wage earners to serve, which skews the makeup of the board and the perspectives that go into its decision making.

The needs of a retired person tend to be different from those of a twenty-something waiting tables to make ends meet.

As for an elected county manager, beyond the monthly meetings, board members also serve on three or four committees—I'll talk about those more later; just know for now that these meet once a month for about two hours during the day. Because these meetings involve county department heads, it makes sense to meet while these employees are still clocked in, rather than forcing them to come back to the office to meet with their elected supervisors. Plus, we'd have to pay them overtime, which would be a hard sell. One of the ways to change this would be to change the structure of the county government and hire a county manager or executive. I'm going to get into the weeds here, but take my hand and it'll all be okay.

This will be easier to grasp if you've ever seen *Parks and Recreation*, with my heroine, the plucky Leslie Knope. (My husband, for the record, is not a Ben Wyatt but a Ron Swanson, if less libertarian.) County government is more like what you see on *Parks* than on *Veep* or *The West Wing*. In fact, it's almost unnerving how accurate *Parks* is. In the show, the government structure of Pawnee, Indiana, includes a city manager, played by the frighteningly handsome Rob Lowe for most of the show's run. Lowe's Chris Traeger is not responsible for making laws or setting policy. His scope of work is to carry out what Pawnee's city council votes on. The manager's job is to supervise all the city employees, their budgets, and requirements from the higher levels of government. In fact, he is a professional with experience in doing just that. In short, Rob Lowe's character makes sure that Pawnee is in compliance with the regulations of the county, the state of Indiana, and the federal government.

Another way to think about it if you haven't seen *Parks and*

Rec—though you should treat yourself—is to picture any retail establishment at a mall. Each Shoe Dept., Limited, and Abercrombie and Fitch has a manager responsible for scheduling his or her employees in accordance with the monies available in the budget while ensuring that the basic duties of selling, stocking, and returning merchandise are performed. The store-level manager doesn't set policy, inventory logistics, or the companywide strategic plan. Those functions are assigned up the chain. (For true wonks: Yes, I know there is a difference between a county manager and a county executive, but that's way more information than the reader needs right now. Seriously, chill.)

Of the fifty-seven counties in New York State (excluding the five in New York City, which have their own wacky structures), only Otsego County has a Board of Representatives and no county manager. This means we're either geniuses who have found the most efficient way to govern and everyone else should jump on board, or the exact opposite of that. Hint: it's that second one.

Rather than have a single contact person for all the routine paperwork and the decisions that need to be made, a department head in Otsego County has *fourteen* bosses, the members of the Board of Reps, most of whom work part time for the county, will be up for election again just about the time they're finally learning the job, and have zero experience running a governmental department.

That last one is important. As we're all finding out—imagine me waving my hands in the air to indicate all that's going on in DC—private-sector skills generally don't transfer well into the public sector. Your business might be a moneymaking machine, but that doesn't mean you know what the Centers for Disease Control requires to keep us safe from Ebola.

So, most of the time that county reps spend in committee

meetings is taken up with the work a manager could otherwise do. Let's say Eve, the head of the Department of Social Services, has to ask the reps on her committee for permission to pay already-budgeted-for bills and to hire, fire, or reclassify an employee or send an employee for training—yes, county board reps have to approve mandated training, even though that training is required by the state. If she doesn't have enough reps in the room to reach a quorum—that is, the number of votes required to pass anything and which is based on some arcane formula I've never been able to wrap my mind around—she can't do anything. Bills won't be paid. People won't be hired, fired, or reclassified. No one will receive training. Instead, Eve has to wait until next month to move that paperwork along.

This wouldn't happen with a county manager, who would be empowered to do all this stuff as long as it fit within already established policy guidelines. Having a county manager would free up time in committee meetings for reps to talk about the challenges and successes the department has had, what they see coming down the planning pike, and how to meet their goals more efficiently. Instead, we have to cram all that into the last few minutes of the meeting, when everyone has started to think about lunch and needs to pee.

There was a very good reason Otsego County hadn't added a county manager: No electeds on the current board wanted to do the heavy lifting involved in making the change. And the lift would be elephant heavy. Someone would need to research how other counties had made the transition and why they chose the style of management they had. Resolutions or a charter change would need to be written. The public would need to be brought on board and, ultimately, would have to agree to whatever path the board proposed. This could take all of a two-year term, if not more, and you still wouldn't have hired anyone to do the job.

After all, if your goal is to get reelected, the status quo is the safest option. But if your goal is to more efficiently serve the people who live in your county and, maybe, just maybe, improve their lives a little, then this change is one that needs to occur.

○ ○ ○

These were my two main talking points: reasonable meeting times and the addition of a county manager system. There were other issues, too. Otsego, like most rural counties across the country, was struggling to provide adequate services to those addicted to opioids and other drugs. It wasn't just recovery agencies and hospitals that were under stress, but the jails and coroners, too. Also, the state's once-lucrative dairy industry was dying, which the county's many dairy farms were feeling. And we could do a heck of a lot more to support our business community and train a twenty-first-century workforce.

But we couldn't do any of that if we had to spend all our time on routine paperwork that could easily have been done by someone else (which John Q. Voter would have known if the meetings were held at a more convenient time).

When I finished writing, I regarded the mailer. As messages went, mine was a keeper. It took me a little bit of work to figure it out, but I got there in the end.

CHAPTER 10

Door After Door, Dollar After Dollar

Once the mailers were printed, I sent them to the 880-ish voters in the district. The extras I carried with me when I went knocking on doors, which had gotten easier but not exactly easy.

Unlike the last time I knocked on the doors in my neighborhood, this time I was after votes rather than signatures, and I was more prepared. Because I can't resist a good arts-and-crafts project, I'd printed out a city map, used highlighters to figure out which streets bordered District Twelve, and then plotted which sections I'd canvass. Once that was done, I broke out my voter spreadsheet, sorted by street, and highlighted which houses were a priority according to my three categories: base, persuadables, and never-gonna-happen-ers.

It was a fine plan, complete with color coding and check marks. I stayed that organized for about a week. After that, I would just reach into my tote bag, pull out a list that looked like it hadn't been worked, and hope for the best. (After the election, when I learned that there are apps for this, I felt more than a little bit bitter. But I did get to spend some quality time with tape and highlighters, so I guess I'm a winner.)

Knocking on doors to hand out campaign materials can be reduced to a decision tree:

1. Does this house have legible house numbers that match your list? Yes? Knock on the door. No? Find the right house.

2. Did someone open the door? Yes? Introduce yourself and say why you are there. Make it clear you are running for county not city. No? Leave a note—"Sorry I missed you! Vote!"—on a flyer and tuck it somewhere they'll see it next time they answer the door. *Do not place it in the mailbox* because that is illegal. Proceed to next house.

3. When you explained that you were running for a county, not city, office, did the person seem to understand the difference? Yes? Explain how voting for you will help shift the power on the board and get some shit done. (Only, don't say "shit.") No? Explain the difference. If they complain about potholes on their street or rowdy college student neighbors, hand over a flyer and write the name of their city council member on the back.

4. Any questions? Yes? Answer them. Duh. No? Thank them for their time, remind them to vote, check them off your list, and repeat the whole process again, and again, and again, until you are so sick of the sound of your own voice that you think you might just lie down on the sidewalk and weep. Then knock on the next door.

◦ ◦ ◦

All this door knocking doesn't guarantee success, of course. Sometimes you do all the work and lose.

In 2018, Elaine DiMasi, a physicist who lives on Long Island, chose to leave her job at the Brookhaven National Lab and run for the U.S. House of Representatives for New York's First District (aka NY1). Elaine was one of six competing in the primary for the Democratic nomination. The way she set herself apart from her competition was to promise to use her background as a scientist to practice evidence-based politics.

Full disclosure: Elaine and I worked at the same summer stock theater when I was in high school and she was starting college. We bonded over a love for Robert Heinlein, Spider Robinson, and a boy who was also working at the summer stock theater. Over the last three decades, we've kept in and (mostly) out of touch. I suspect she was just as shocked as I was when we each learned that the other was getting involved in politics.

I gave her a call to talk about her experiences and ask why a gainfully employed physicist would take a risk on getting elected.

"It had everything to do with knowing that the number of scientists in Congress had decreased from three eight years ago to just one physicist now," Elaine says. "People now walk into the Chamber with a snowball in their hand and talk about climate."

Trump's election made running for office make sense for Elaine, not because she was angry (like, say, me), but because she realized that other people would be angry enough to contribute their money and time to a relatively unknown candidate. With a Democratic voter or anyone who understood how government works, she figured she could use her twenty-one-year résumé with a national lab to gain the public's trust in her work ethic. With voters who just couldn't pull the lever for Hillary Clinton, Elaine planned to point out that she's not a politician. This path was full of possibility.

Elaine traveled to DC for a few workshops on the legal and financial logistics of running for office, but discovered that one of the harder parts was community organization. She watched other scientists across the county run, "and I saw what they had to do to get people organized into teams and lay the groundwork," she says. "I watched, and I learned a little, but I didn't really have it when push came to shove."

But the hardest part was raising enough money to support a House campaign. "It's completely relentless," she says. "You can't just host a fund-raiser party. You have to call ten people and twist their arms really hard to be cohosts. You have to demand they bring five hundred dollars or a thousand dollars, and you have to demand that they come with twenty guests, and the guests have to be confronted with a hundred-and-twenty-five-dollar ticket. You have to just keep on telling people to do more, more, more, more—more than they want to do. And you never get to stop."

That's what gets lost in all the Run for Something and She Should Run dialogue, which is so understandably loud in the post-Trump political landscape. When you are seeking a state or federal office, raising large amounts of money and continuously recruiting volunteers is an all-consuming job.

"It's hard to have nothing to do all day but ask other people to help you," Elaine says. "There was so little I could do with my own two hands except dial a phone and ask for help. And so, I didn't always do that—then a week has gone by, and you've missed your chance to call a hundred people a day. That's seven hundred people who are not helping you. But I would not have really learned what was and wasn't possible without jumping in and doing things.

"That's kind of how the whole race went. 'Oh, I don't have enough money. I don't have enough people. Yet there's enough money to keep the lights on and enough true believers among the volunteers that we can do the next step anyway.'"

Elaine and her team believed there was a possibility she

could squeak out a win on primary day. She didn't. Business-man Perry Gershon won the Democratic line and took on Republican Lee Zeldin in the November race. Zeldin won by more than 11,000 votes.

That doesn't mean that Elaine regrets the experience. She learned a lot about herself and the political world. One of the best parts of running for office, she says, was knowing she had an impact by having the most insightful answer in a forum or hearing her words repeated by someone else. The worst part was the constant feeling of failure, she says, "Because nothing is ever enough."

Another hard part, when you've spent most of your life analyzing data, is working a crowd. When she lost the primary, "one of the incredible bits of relief I had was to go to a shopping mall for jeans. It didn't matter what expression I had on my face, because no one had to like me, because I wasn't running for elective office."

Given how challenging she found some aspects of cam-paigning, she's not sure she wants to run again. "My strengths are understanding the complexities of crazy data coming at me," she says. "Maybe the job is for me to be an operative, but I will never be the one who can walk through a hall, shake every hand, and remember every face."

What gives her hope is how willing people were to get engaged in the political process, no matter how rough their lives were. "They found time to try to campaign for their can-didate instead of just sitting in front of the TV and bitching. I admire the people I've met. It's hard to imagine turning off all the bad news and going back to my nice job. I no longer think that being a scientist is quite enough. But I'm also, right now, not convinced of my skills for what I tried to do. I need time to figure it out," she says.

"What gives me hope is that more people are learning how to go out in the real world and talk to each other in person," she says. "At the same time, the internet gives us a way to have it be coordinated and not really just a bunch of individuals in a maze, in the dark with candles."

◦ ◦ ◦

When Elaine and I talked about campaigning, we both hit on the same analogy: it's like a video game. "We had these doors that we had to hit. It wasn't every door. They were kind of spread out because they were targeted voters. And I'm like, 'This is a really slow game of *Pac-Man*.'

"I don't even get a power-up," I said. "Who gives me the power-up? I don't even get a cherry."

"There's no power-up," she agreed. "You have to quit and go get a pretzel at the mall. That's it."

◦ ◦ ◦

Without a Trump presidency, I wouldn't have run. Paradoxically, that same presidency made certain parts of my political life much easier even as they made everything else in the country harrowing. After Trump, the Democratic Party woke up, rubbed its eyes, and hit the ground like a rabid bear. Anti-Trumpers from all parties were making money rain on us. Those without financial means were volunteering all the time they could manage. I benefited from both.

When I put together my artsy-crafty map, I chunked off a couple of blocks that would be covered by a group of energetic high-schoolers/college kids who wanted to take some action but were either too young to vote or too broke to donate money, or both. One Saturday morning, I handed off a stack of flyers and they did the rest, knocking on doors and getting the word out. By that point in the fall—this was maybe mid-October—my enthusiasm was low and diving even lower. Their enthusiasm, however, more than made up for it.

Then, the next weekend, they helped out another Dem candidate, then another. It was like a small invading force whose weapons were a positive attitude, pink cheeks, and flexible knees. One of the ringleaders, Maguire Benton, continued to work on campaigns after the 2017 election and is now in office in Cooperstown. Another, Clark Oliver, worked for a state assembly candidate and is, as I write, campaigning for a seat on the Otsego County board.

In short: the kids are all right, and they are just getting started.

I kept up my end, too, and picked off houses whenever I had a couple of free hours. Maybe half the houses I visited opened their doors to me, which was nice. Of that half, maybe half again knew that the county election was coming up and could articulate what they saw as the county's biggest problems. Every now and again, one of my potential voters clearly knew a lot more about an issue than I did, and I had to admit that it would be something I'd have to study.

That part was similar to teaching, which I did as an adjunct at SUNY Oneonta for ten years before moving into the alumni office. My teaching routine was pretty simple: I'd take attendance, do my little song-and-dance about that day's topic, remind the students that it would probably be on the test, and then ask for questions. Every couple of months, I'd get one that stumped me. Rather than bluster my way through, though, I'd make a note, say I'd find out, and then report back. To a student, they all seemed surprised that a teacher would admit ignorance. I'm always surprised when they don't.

∘ ∘ ∘

One question still stumps me, and it's one that much better policy minds than mine are flailing at with nearly no success: "What will you do to combat the opioid epidemic in the county?"

The asker was an acquaintance, one who'd retired from a well-paying, well-respected position. She told me about her son, who'd been struggling with addiction for years and had the rehab and court records to match. I can't stress this part enough, however: she could have been any parent of any child in any corner of the county. Addiction doesn't care where you live or who your parents are or how much education you have. Opioids especially seem to cut across class, even if our treatment of the addicts remains contingent on how much they can pay. But that's another problem.

In 2016, 218 unique people with an opioid addiction had sought treatment in Otsego County. In this usage, "unique" means that the person is new to the county. A person can seek treatment any number of times—but they will count in the statistics only the first time. This number doesn't give you a good sense of how busy the clinics are. It doesn't tell you the stress that the epidemic is placing on the jail, where half the residents at any given time are there because of drug-related crimes. At the time I ran for office, jail-based drug treatment had only recently been fully implemented, which meant that over the last ten years, a lot of corrections officers were doing work they really weren't prepared for.

The epidemic has side effects you might not even think of. The increased number of overdoses increases the number of calls to 911. The use of NARCAN is saving lives, yes, but doing nothing to change the underlying behavior, which means EMTs are seeing the same people again and again. The increased number of overdoses is also increasing the numbers of calls our coroners make. They have to sign off on every unattended death and are therefore spending less time in nursing homes and more time in rural homes.

The opioid epidemic is chewing into our economic development, too. There could be more tourist-focused attractions (hotels, restaurants, and shops) near the Hall of Fame and baseball camps. There could be more light industry along the I-88 corridor. While there are many reasons these projects have been slow to start, one of the many is that potential employees aren't going to pass a drug test.

And why should they? For so many of them, the safety net system keeps losing funding, and people who need help fall through the cracks. When you live out in farm country, which most of Otsego County is, you need a reliable car to get to a job because public transportation is either not useful or non-existent. What incentive is there to stay on a sober path if you don't have many options to be a productive member of society and the few options you do have are terrible? Why not just give in? At least opioids take the pain away—at first, anyway. It gets ugly after that.

There is no single answer to "What will you do to combat the opioid epidemic in the county?" All we can do right now is keep throwing ideas at it and hope something breaks through. Like many answers to questions about the government, this honest answer isn't satisfying.

◦ ◦ ◦

Apart from the occasional hard question, knocking on doors was perfectly fine. It's not my favorite activity, but if you want to understand a place, it's something that needs to be done.

No one slammed the door in my face or chased me off their porch with a broom. I had only two (exceedingly polite) encounters with voters who had no intention of voting for me. One simply said, "I'm a lifelong Republican." I reminded him to vote, scurried off his doorstep, and made a note on my list. The other said, "I went to high school with [your opponent] and will be voting for him." I reminded him to vote, scurried off his screened-in front porch, and made a note on my list.

You can run for office and spend nothing on the endeavor if you have name recognition or are running unopposed—or, I guess, if you are just running to run and don't care if you win. I cared.

In this part of New York, you can spend five hundred dollars on flyers to hand out plus a couple dozen lawn signs and likely do okay. It really depends on the rest of the field. If your opponent is well funded, an incumbent, a local hero, and so on, you are going to need to spend more.

I spent more.

When I tallied it at the end, I took in $3,687 and sent out $3,277, which left $410 that I carried over for 2019 (and have had to report to the state every six months). I would have spent that last four hundred bucks but simply ran out of items to spend it on.

In hindsight, I could have done it for much less, maybe $1,200, but it's hard to know what actually moved the needle and what was a waste. The old adage about advertising is that 50 percent of it doesn't work; you just never know which 50 percent. I did ignore the advertising adage of selling the sizzle and not the steak. Sizzle is what got us into our current predicament.

Well, sizzle and Russia.

Before I get into details about where the money went and how I got it in the first place, a caveat: your town/city/county/parish/township/etc. has its own election economy. It will be a small fraction of what it takes to campaign on a state level and a rounding error on what it takes nationally. While the numbers I'm giving you here are unique to this part of New York

State, know that running for a local office takes a small amount of cash and a lot of time and moxie.

One hundred yard signs cost four hundred dollars and were one of the biggest pains in the ass of the whole campaign. My husband and I spent hours inserting the metal holder parts into the plastic sign parts. One hundred yard signs is a lot of yard signs, by the way. I could have gotten fifty and been just fine. Yard signs are a one-time expense as long as you remember not to put a date on them. I'll use the same signs in 2019. And if I'm feeling kicky, I'll add a "Reelect" sticker.

Once assembled, the signs had to be distributed, which meant asking everyone I knew in Oneonta to stick one in their yard, regardless of whether they were in my district. I gave a sign to anyone who asked. Since there are four districts in the city, I figured I had a one-in-four chance of a potential voter spotting a sign no matter where it wound up. Oneonta just isn't that big.

The harder part was sticking them in the public places beside busy roads, where campaign signs pop up every election season like mushrooms after a spring rain. Knowing where to put them wasn't the challenge. Pulling into the breakdown or bike lane, zipping out to a muddy median, planting a sign, and zipping back to my car was. It's a wonder more candidates don't get run over.

Once again, I was saved by the youngsters who volunteered to help. Those with little fear of playing in traffic took over. To accompany signs from the two other newbie candidates in the city, I handed over twenty-five of mine. Forty-eight hours later, my signs were legion. About a week after that, my opponent and/or his enthusiastic volunteers put his signs directly in front of mine in the most visible spots.

My first response was to rant about it to my husband. We've been together for more than twenty-five years—yes, we started dating as infants—and he knows to wait for me to wind down before offering comment. When I finally made it to the stage where I kept repeating "I mean . . ." and sighing, he asked, "What do you want to do about it?"

"I don't want to do anything about it, because then my time will be taken up with some stupid sign-shuffling dance," I said. "But I should do something, right? I should go all Lebowski-y, like, 'This aggression will not stand, man.' But it's not, like, illegal, just irritating. It's the spirit of the act, you know?"

"Maybe it's a power move because someone sees you as a threat."

"No one sees me as a threat," I said. "I think it's just general dickishness, and do I want to take the time to fight dickishness with more dickishness?"

I did not, mostly because lawn sign logistics was something I'd already spent way too much time on. I will, however, complain about it after the fact. In the moment, though, I let it go and used the time I would have spent shuffling signs around to knock on doors.

Printing flyers and postcards cost about $275. Processing and postage were another $390.

Ads on Facebook cost $57. I had two different ones: a generic reminder about the election and a specific visual about me. Because Facebook provides analytics, I could see how many people had some interaction with each ad, and discovered that it cost 25 cents per exposure—which is fine, I guess, though definitely not a substitute for other types of advertising.

Speaking of, Oneonta is one of the remaining small communities that still has a local daily newspaper—well, almost daily. There's a singular weekend edition rather than a Saturday and a Sunday. (I almost wrote here that it is a thriving local paper, but I don't know that any local papers are thriving right now. So, I'll say it's hanging in there.)

I placed black-and-white ads in the daily paper and a full-color spectacular in the weekend edition during the week leading up to Election Day. The total cost was my largest expenditure: $1,475. I wasn't going to spend a lot on newspaper ads because I wasn't sure I would reach anyone who didn't already know who I was and that an election was coming up, but about a week before I committed to an ad contract, Oneonta's mayor, Gary Herzig, sent a surprising chunk of change my way. I thanked him and mentioned that I didn't have a use for it. He looked at me as if I were a loon—what politician can't spend money?—and suggested I do more of whatever I was already doing. So, I sent it to the local paper.

The Otsego County Democratic Committee also placed ads for the entire slate of candidates up for election in the region in both the daily and the weekly papers. I chipped in $300.

Perhaps the smartest check I wrote was to Rapid Resist, an organization that sends out mass texts for blue causes. I spent $150 for the organization to text every voter in my district with a valid cell number on Election Day. The message included a simple reminder for them to go vote and the location of the polling place. I honestly think that right there was what made the difference between my winning and losing in 2017. Voters were looking for a way to express their distaste for the undrained DC swamp. This local election was a good first step.

CHAPTER 11

Finance Forms, Fundraising Platforms, Debate Stage

Asking for money, like knocking on doors, never gets easy. It only becomes slightly less hard with time.

Initially, I had zero intention of raising funds at all. In New York, you can self-fund up to one thousand dollars and not have to report anything, which had its appeal. I'd heard rumors that the election finance paperwork was complicated and time-consuming. As a one-woman operation, I figured that opting to spend less money and time was the more efficient course.

Only one problem: given the national political situation, folks were fired up and ready to open their wallets. And the wrong answer to someone standing in front of you with a checkbook is "No, thanks. I'm good." Happily accept whatever is freely offered, even if it means a filing headache later. Yet heed my warning: keep careful track of who and how much.

One sunny afternoon, Dave, the local Democratic Party member whose bright idea got me into this whole mess, held a fund-raiser at his house. We sent invites far and wide. His wife and kids made tasty snacks. Beer and wine flowed freely. I collected my last few signatures to get on the ballot and a couple hundred dollars in checks as well.

The problem was that I hadn't opened a separate campaign checking account, and had no idea how to do so legally; neither did my local credit union, which wanted a whole stack of forms I didn't have. The local bank knew it could be done, given that it had done it for other candidates, but no one I talked to had a solid idea how. After a few phone calls to the banking bigwigs, we figured out there was a number I needed from the state. The mystery was how to get one.

Since I had to drive out to the County Board of Elections office, which is located in something called the Meadows Office Building, which, indeed, overlooks a meadow, I figured I'd ask them about the number. Despite their efficiency with logging and sorting my signature sheets, the folks behind the official desk weren't sure about all the finance forms and mysterious numbers that banks might need. Candidates usually file a CF-05, they told me, so I did that.

It was not, as it turns out, the right form. What followed was a *Brazil*-esque series of phone calls, trips to the post office and a notary, a few more phone calls, photocopies of every piece of ID I had, a trip to the bank and another notary, and finally the magical number was mine.

(Short version of an incredibly long, boring story: After a brief flirtation with a CF-03, which had been recommended by the first person I talked to in Albany, my second call to the capital made it clear that I needed to commit to a CF-04. The CF-05 I had at first filed was but a distant memory, and we shall think of each other fondly. Also, for the record, if you can't deal with this sort of bureaucratic hassle without blowing a gasket, public service might not be for you.)

Banking issues sorted, I deposited my first round of checks, most of which had come from friends and neighbors. I duly wrote thank-you notes to all. What I wanted to write was "Let me express my sincere gratitude for the contribution to my campaign because it implies that you think I might have a chance at winning this and/or are further encouraging my delusion that this is a good idea. I promise not to spend this on malt liquor and beef jerky." Instead, I went with something like "Thanks. I'll use this to fight for greater accountability in our county's government."

That mystical number from the New York State Board of Elections also unlocked an online funding tool for me: Crowdpac, a platform for left-leaning candidates to raise money online. It's perfect for smaller offices because those candidates don't have money to hire an IT department to manage all the record-keeping and credit card processing. With my Crowdpac address, I was able to nudge friends and family to send a couple of dollars my way, and the site took care of tracking what needed to be tracked.

This online engine is similar to Crowdrise, which charities frequently use. When I ran the New York City Marathon, I raised money for Every Mother Counts, an organization started by supermodel Christy Turlington to call attention to how dangerous it can be for a woman to give birth. It's a global problem, from sub-Saharan Africa to the United States. The organization's cause is one I wholeheartedly support, even if I've never met Christy herself (though I imagine I'd feel very short and lament my nondewy skin if I did). We don't pay enough attention to what mothers need, which is a soapbox issue for another day.

My point, and I do have one, is that I had some familiarity using a portal like Crowdpac. I have also conditioned the people in my immediate orbit to help fund harebrained schemes. That doesn't mean I find it easy to ask, mind.

Fortunately, I have friends with no such issues. One of them lives in Iowa and is a lobbyist for progressive causes. We met at a running retreat—yes, there are running retreats—and kept in touch over the years. Her name is Kate, and she has the most lustrous dark hair I've ever seen.

Iowa Kate offered two pieces of advice: first, the only way to win is to get in the game, and second, campaigns need money. Once I had a Crowdpac site, she mentioned to all our shared friends that small amounts of money make a difference and that I was too polite to beg—both statements are true—and because of her words, the donations rolled in. Locals donated, too, even a few I'd never met. I wrote every one of them a thank-you note, which the Trailblazers' workshop had taught me was important.

The Crowdpac platform kept track of all the whos and wheres and how muches. Every month, I had to block off an afternoon to enter it all into New York State's online campaign finance widget to report it. Said widget would be charming in its retro-ness if it weren't so user-hostile. But I persevered, mostly because not entering all the numbers could have led to unpleasant interactions between me and the legal system.

I wish I had magical advice for asking for donations. For me, it's like knocking on doors. The more you do it, the easier it gets, but it will never be easy.

Here we come at last to the part of running for office that terrified me even more than asking people for money. No, not the little dogs who wanted to bite me when I was in their yard. No, not putting an eye out with the stabby end of a yard sign. What scared me most was the debate.

Our local branch of the League of Women Voters, a national organization that is strictly nonpartisan, holds a candidate panel discussion every year. In our county, these are a big deal. A bigwig from the daily paper and one from the small weekly come to ask questions. The halls where the panel discussions are held fill up quickly, and every so often, things get heated.

Three of us running for city districts would be at the table. Two of us would be seated next to the Republican incumbents we were running against. The third Democrat and her Libertarian opponent would fill out the panel. The fourth candidate running for a city seat would be in the audience. He was the incumbent and running unchallenged.

For the entire month of October, I had wake-up-wanting-to-barf-level dread about this event, which is weird. When I taught, I had few qualms about facing a roomful of students. When my first two books were published, I never sweated a reading or a Q&A. And I routinely give a New Year's Eve sermon/reflection/lecture at our Unitarian Universalist church. But sitting at a table next to the man whose job I wanted to take and talking about issues of which I had only the most rudimentary understanding gave me a case of the freak-outs. Give me an opportunity for rambling stories and humorous asides, and I'm there before you even finish the request. But ask me to verbalize coherent thoughts about every part of the county's system, and you'll have to dig me out from under my bed.

Still, I put on my big girl underpants and agreed to do it.

In between knocking on doors, doing my actual job, keeping track of my offspring, and making sure our house wasn't declared a FEMA site, I crammed for the debate with the help of current Democratic board members. They had a tendency to wander deep into the weeds when briefing me on what they had identified as the most pressing issues from within the halls of power. Looking back at my notes, I see that those jaunts into the dandelions made sense (except for a note that simply read "Local monster," which I still haven't figured out). I approached these cram sessions as I had my high school statistics class: I just wrote everything down and hoped it would make sense before the test.

My debate notes hit on issues that could apply to many counties with a similar rural–small city mix: Small farms are vital and need our help. Tourism is key, and we need more of it, but never, ever at the expense of the region's natural beauty. Business needs to grow, but not if that growth requires fossil fuels or a gas compressor substation. And jobs, jobs, jobs—but make sure they are good ones that pay a living wage and that don't take farmers away from farms or damage the tourism industry or require more cars on the road.

And this is why it's hard to be straightforward when you're running for public office. Every single answer will tick someone off. If you say you are pro-tourism and pro-business, clearly you are anti-farm and anti-environment. If you try to avoid seeming pro or anti anything you are considered unable to make hard choices and are a flip-flopper.

When I taught persuasion in an Intro to Communications class, I explained that compromise isn't the solution to a conflict where everyone gets exactly what he or she wants. Instead, it's the state where everyone is equally unhappy. I could be wrong, but a promise to distribute unhappiness equally doesn't seem like it will win hearts and minds in the political arena.

The only idea everyone agrees on is how odious it would be to raise taxes, despite the simple math that shows that more money into the system is the only way to get more money out of it. Some insist that we should grow the tax base by capitalizing on our tourism industry, but we shouldn't do that if it has any environmental impact or increases wear and tear on the roads. And again, the great wheel spins.

I've already mentioned a couple of the topics that were likely to come up in the panel discussion, such as broadband and opioids. The list also included our solid waste and recycling fees, raises for county employees, upgrades to the jail and other county buildings, so-called bomb trucks, our solar farm, Otsego Now (the county's industrial development agency), and the animal shelter. By the time I was done making my lists, I had six pages of thumbnail descriptions of each issue and a rising sense of dread. I spent the entire week before the debate on a newfangled slimming plan: I lost five pounds because I was too nauseated to eat. (Worry not. I gained them all back plus a few.)

A day or two before the event, the organizer left me a message: my opponent had never responded to the League of Women Voters' calls to attend the debate. The LWV has a strict no-empty-chair policy, which meant that if he didn't show, I couldn't be onstage. "Would it be okay," the organizer asked, "if we waited twenty-four more hours before canceling your part of the event?"

"No worries," I said. "I'm very disappointed that I may not have the chance to speak, but I understand."

Reader, I lied. I wasn't disappointed at all, and I spent about an hour taking deep breaths and enjoying my chill. That's about how long it took before the organizer called back to let me know that my opponent was in and we'd both get to say our respective pieces the next day.

◦ ◦ ◦

On the late October day of the debate, I showed up to the campus banquet room in a burnt-orange skirt, a grown-up striped blouse, and black leather boots. The six of us were seated behind a long table facing rows of chairs. Two newspaper reporters/editors were off to our right. There was a lectern for the moderator, a professor from Hartwick College's political science department, whom I sort of knew from dinner parties at my RN friend Kate's house. Like I said, in small towns, you really have only two degrees of separation from anyone else.

Maybe fifty people were in the audience, and the event was recorded for anyone who couldn't make it. Also in the audience were my father and my husband. I wasn't entirely sure I wanted them there—I always find it hard to remember that I'm a damn grown-up around my dad—but I wasn't sure I didn't want them there, either. I am a puzzle.

The one thing I was certain I didn't want there were my kids. My daughter would have spent the entire time staring daggers at me for making her listen to something so freaking boring. My son is an upstager and would therefore have found a way to make the audience laugh, while I stared daggers at him until he wrapped it up. He has a nimble wit, actually, but with no sense of when he's testing an audience's patience. We're hoping he will someday figure out how to use this power for good.

My opponent and I formally introduced ourselves to each other, even though we'd probably met before somewhere at some point, and sat down to wait for go time. I read and reread my notes in the hope that I could cram one more fact about our solid waste tip fees into my already full-to-bursting skull.

Then the discussion was called to order, and we began.

Each candidate was given two minutes at the beginning to set up his or her bona fides. This was the only part of the night when I felt fully on top of things, given that I had been able to write my remarks out beforehand and practice them a few times. After a quick paragraph about how long I'd lived there and why we'd stayed, I moved on to my main points:

> [E]ven wonderful places face challenges. Right now, it feels like the county's growth has stagnated. Folks

in Otsego County keep hearing about unrealized master plans that will bring investment into the area from the outside.

Maybe a better plan would be to grow what is already here. We can make local business stronger by training a twenty-first-century workforce who can fill living wage jobs. Given the climate in DC, we need to make sure our people have access to quality, affordable health care—and protect the health care sector itself, which is one of the top three employers in Otsego. There may already be plans to do that. But what goes on at the county government level seems to exist in a vacuum. Plans go in but don't ever seem to come out. It's hard to say why from the perspective of an average citizen.

That's why I decided to run. I've made part of my living as a professional communicator by understanding how processes such as student scholarships work and simply explaining how they affect all of us. Life here can be even more enjoyable with an energetic county government that tells its voters what it is doing to help them.

Then I thanked the League of Women Voters, the members of the audience, and all the ships at sea, and waited for the questions to begin.

Here's where I would love to give you a blow-by-blow of every question asked and every response given. I will not be doing that, mostly because I had some sort of out-of-body experience and remember very little of what happened next. I remember a question about arts funding, which came up because the Libertarian believed the government should pay for nothing other than the military. That might be the only question that made my feet feel like they were on anything other than quicksand, which is why I remembered it.

I've looked back on what was reported afterward. Erin Jerome, a journalist for the (almost) daily local paper, captured a small sliver of the event:

> The candidates generally agreed on several issues, including the need to hire a board-appointed county executive to help oversee the city's [technically, county's] $105 million budget.
>
> "We need to put this to bed," Gelbsman said, adding that he has supported the idea for several years, and that the board representatives "are consumed with managing department heads."
>
> Martini expressed disappointment in the board's initiatives to invigorate the economy and revitalize the city. "Plans go in but they don't ever seem to come out," she said.

About the best that can be said about the debate is that I didn't do anything remarkably silly. I didn't curse or have a wardrobe malfunction. My husband summed it up best. When I saw him afterward, he said, "That's just really not your venue." Truer words have not been spoken.

In short, I survived, and we now were only two weeks away from Election Day.

CHAPTER 12

Election Day

I would be lying if I said I was my best self on the first Tuesday in November. The anger that had wanted to consume me whole had been replaced by exhaustion I carried around like overstuffed luggage. My boss seemed surprised that I came in to work on Election Day, as if there was something politics related I should be doing instead. But there was nothing for me to do. The local party takes care of poll watching: at each polling station, a party volunteer sits behind the election officials and writes down each person's name as they are given a ballot. Each poll watcher then reports their names to the county headquarters. As the day goes on, any Democrats who haven't yet done their civic duty are called with a friendly reminder to do so. This is perfectly legal, by the way. It is also (allegedly) something the local Republicans are very, very good at.

So, if getting voters to the polls was not my problem, what was I supposed to do with myself?

Instead of pacing around my living room and irritating the dog, I went to work. But there I paced around my office and irritated my coworkers. Occasionally, I stared at alumni magazine page proofs, marked up edits, and wondered why my grammar was so awful. (This is my routine for every issue. I marvel at how anyone thinks I know how English works, because I clearly don't, based on the proofreader's marks.)

Nearly every person I saw on Tuesday asked the same question: "Are you going to win?"

My stock answer was "I've done everything I can, given the limits of my energy and pocketbook. Tonight, I'll either forget all about the work of the last six months and sleep the sleep of the just or discover that I have a whole new set of problems."

That was my stock answer for people who didn't know me, mind. My answer for friends was "Fuck if I know." Because, seriously, fuck if I knew. County races don't get breathless horserace coverage in the media. When in my presence, people said that I had their vote, but that meant nothing. And when my mother-in-law asked what the polls were saying, I laughed out loud. At this level, no one can afford to pay for a poll. The election itself is the poll.

At lunch, I drove to my polling location, a performing arts center that has struggled from the moment it opened fifteen years ago, which is a city problem and not a county problem. The weather was decent for an early November day in the Northeast: blustery and gray but not actively raining. The performing arts center wasn't nearly as busy as it had been during the previous November's presidential election, but there were two people in front of me for ballot pickup.

Because the town is small, I didn't even have to give the older—well, older than me—woman my name. She flipped to the *M*s in the official book. I saw that my dad had been in earlier, because on the line below my name, I saw the same signature I'd seen on countless report cards. I signed in, too, and was handed a paper ballot. My heart started racing because *my name was on the ballot*. This wasn't news, but *seriously, what was I thinking*?

I walked as calmly as I could to the rows of partitioned-off, shaky tables where voters use the attached-to-the-table off-brand Sharpie to mark their choices. I took a good long look at the ballot, briefly pondered taking a selfie with it, then filled in my choices for a couple of countywide proposals, a state supreme court justice, the county treasurer (there was only one candidate for each), and the county coroners.

Then I got to the District Twelve county rep choice. I made sure to fill in the oval next to my name. I double-checked, just to make sure I hadn't had a brain freeze and filled in my opponent's bubble, which would have been embarrassing. But, no. Even my body knew I was the best choice for the office and had acted in concert with my brain.

Then I walked to big ballot scanner, fed mine into its maw, saw that the machine's screen read "Ballot Cast," got my "I Voted" sticker, and went back to the office.

After that, there wasn't much to do between dinner and 9 p.m., which is when the polls closed and all the city candidates would meet up at a local bar. My husband and I decided to watch the national returns on TV and wait for good news. Remember, this was 2017. Democrats hadn't flipped the U.S. House yet. No one really knew if all the fresh Democratic energy would convert into votes. Scott and I kept our eyes on the screen and held our breaths for Virginia. The Commonwealth would be a bellwether. When seats started going Democratic, we exhaled. For the first time in months, the knots of tension in my shoulders relaxed long enough for me to realize how tight the races actually were. There was still a lot of work to do, but the momentum had shifted, if a little, and that was enough.

Frankly, once I saw the results coming out of Virginia, I was good with whatever would be my fate. I had done what I'd set out to do: I had channeled my anger into something productive and done my small part to make sure that someone challenged the local Republican incumbent. He didn't just get to have the seat because the Democrats failed to fight. He had to earn it.

It sounds weird, I know, but as my husband and I were gathering ourselves up to go out after dinner on a school night, I realized I was cool with losing—indeed, 100 percent A-okay with it. Running for office would always be a thing I had done. The result was inconsequential.

Just as we were getting our coats on, one of the kids yelled from the upstairs bathroom, "It's going everywhere!" Experienced parents know this is one of the few unignorable phrases, right up there with "My tummy feels funny" and "Where are the matches?"

Our toilet celebrated the end of the campaign by clogging itself so firmly that all manner of ick was bubbling up and out. It was, indeed, going everywhere. The kids, who were old enough to do something useful, opted instead to stand there and watch the poo waterfall, rather than grab some towels and dam the tide.

Scott and I rolled into the results party fresh from this level-two biohazard spill. With us was my friend Jenny, who had grown up in Iowa and, until she was out of college, didn't realize that one didn't actually get to meet every potential presidential candidate at church suppers. Waiting for us at the bar was nurse Kate and acupuncturist Laura—you haven't met her; she's lovely. Also, there was every politically associated person within a ten-mile radius. So, maybe thirty people?

Beers were bought. I grabbed a Sprite.

Everyone who passed asked, "How are you feeling?"

I answered each time, "Great, actually!" Because I felt great. Soon I would know my fate and get to lie down for a bit. What could be better?

If you're thinking that the bar TV was turned to some kind of local news ticker, reporting on the votes as they were counted, you are a very silly person who has never lived in a small city. The local news stations are based in cities at least an hour away—in Binghamton, Utica, and Syracuse—and they didn't care at all about real-time tracking of our results. Instead, we had Andrew Stammel, a current county rep, with his cell phone. He was getting texts from where the votes were being tabulated. When there were updates, he'd raise his voice over the din and announce them.

Like all the county reps, Andrew was also up for reelection that year. His race was expected to be close but not a nail-biter. The powers that be seemed 90 percent certain his rear end would occupy the seat for the next two years. After 2016, nothing felt like a walkover. Some of us—okay, maybe just me—were concerned about the races in which there was only one person on the ballot. What if there'd been a huge write-in campaign for someone's pet chicken? What then? (By the way, Andrew is a real-life Paul Bradford from Neil Simon's play *Barefoot in the Park*. The stage version is superior, but the movie adaptation with Jane Fonda and Robert Redford is great, too. Redford plays Bradford, a young lawyer. Before they're married, the Fonda character wonders if Paul sleeps in his button-down shirt and tie. "Only for very formal sleeps," Paul replies. That's Andrew.)

One by one, Andrew called out results. He prevailed. Most of the other races came out about as expected. Incumbents from both parties kept their seats. No chickens were elected. Three races were coming down to the wire, and one of them was mine.

The other two would wind up being decided two weeks later, when the absentee ballots were opened. In one, the incumbent won by 17 votes. In the other, the newbie Democrat won by 5 votes. If five people had decided that their vote didn't matter and had stayed home, the county board would still be under Republican control. I'm sure it would have been fine, but I'm glad those five people made the trip so that the county didn't have to find out.

I've been told the expression on my face the moment Andrew told me I'd won was priceless. If it mirrored what was going on in my brain, my face displayed a mix of pure disbelief, excitement, vindication, pride, and terror. Kate, Laura, Jenny, my husband, and I all threw ourselves into a giant group hug. I did my best not to pour the soda in my hand down anyone's back.

Scott whispered "You did it" in my ear. He followed that up with "Now what?"—a running joke between us that started when our first child could not stop watching *Finding Nemo*. The movie ends with the tropical fish heroes trapped in plastic bags bobbing along in the ocean. "Now what?" one of them says, as they realize that their cunning plan got them their freedom, technically, but they had no plan for what would happen next.

In all fairness, I had no idea "now what." What mattered most right that second was that my own daring plan had worked.

The rest of the night went by in a blur. Technically, my race couldn't officially be called in my favor because I was ahead by only 23 votes in this first count and twenty-four absentee ballots had been sent out. Of those twenty-four, sixteen had come back already, but the other eight had ten days to trickle their way into the Board of Elections. If those eight showed up and all twenty-four went for my opponent, then he'd be the winner.

Again, we were all 90 percent certain I'd won (even Andrew, who tends to hedge his bets, what with being a lawyer and all), but the specter of 2016 would not stop haunting us.

What convinced me that I could trust the night's results

was our drive home from the bar. We'd passed dozens of my opponent's lawn signs as we were driving there. Now, just a couple of hours later, they had all vanished like free food at a college picnic.

By the time the dust had cleared, the absentee ballots had been tallied, and the machines had been inventoried, the official vote was 204 to 175. Of my 204 votes, 178 were on the Democratic line and 26 were on the Working Families line. I don't know what to make of that information, but I suspect that some voters just couldn't blacken the bubble on a Democrat's line, or the votes had been simply random, or both.

Once I wrapped my head around them, the numbers revealed a few more insights. In terms of total votes cast, 2017 spanked the turnout of past years. In my district, total turnout started at a low of 270 in 2011 and rose steadily to 315 in 2015. In 2017, 380 voters showed up, which is a 20 percent increase in just two years.

I'd like to chalk that up to my sheer magnetism as a candidate, even though I live with myself and know that can't possibly be true. No, prevailing political winds lifted my sails. In my district, the intense dislike for Trump and the Republican Party's pro-discrimination policies was palpable. People wanted to do something about all the chaos coming out of DC, and this particular election was the first chance they'd had to demonstrate their anger. Of course, the local Republican Party didn't do itself any favors by hosting Roger Stone for its summer 2017 fund-raiser. For a few of my constituents, that event was the last straw.

I don't know if I would have won the seat in 2015. I certainly wouldn't have run in the first place, because I didn't know why it was important to do so. There also wouldn't have been nearly as many open checkbooks and willing volunteers.

CHAPTER 13

Swearing In and Setting Up (Or, All the Responsibility and None of the Power)

Between Election Eve in 2017 and my January 1, 2018, swearing in, I had to collect my dang yard signs, which was a challenge. Just when I thought I'd gotten them all, one more would creep out from behind a hedge or pop up in a backyard. It was a sign-based Easter egg hunt. The number I found would never equal the number I put out. Eventually, it started to snow, and I decided that I couldn't collect what I couldn't see under all the drifts.

I had more to worry about by then, anyway, such as all the paperwork and preliminary meetings and more paperwork and a training day in Albany. Plus, the college was sprinting into the end of the semester, which is always madness. And there were Thanksgiving and Christmas to deal with, to say nothing of reintroducing myself to my kids and husband, whom I'd neglected for six months.

In roughly six weeks, I had to make the transition from running for office to occupying one. This second part of my unexpected political career had to be easier than the first part. Now I'd just sit in meetings, read stuff, and vote. How hard could that be?

Yeah, I can hear the laughing, too.

○ ○ ○

My first swearing-in ceremony was held on a bitterly cold afternoon in Hartwick College's chapel. The view from there never fails to take my breath away, even on a day when the freezing temps make it hard for you to catch your breath in the first place. From there, you can see the valley in which Oneonta is snuggled. Allegedly, the name Oneonta comes from the Iroquois *Onaanta*, which translates as "City of/in the Hills." Given what the incoming white settlers did to the native tribes here, we will never know if this is accurate. Still, the view is pleasing, even if you don't want to linger too much in the outdoors to take it in.

The event was arranged by one of the incumbent board members and a few of the other party higher-ups. There were a couple of swearing-ins taking place all over the county, but this one focused on the city-area elected officials, including those for the town board, county reps, and city council members. The mayor gave a State of the City speech, which was perfectly adequate. Our mayor is a solid guy but not known for his soaring oratory. To quote my husband, it does not play to his strengths.

My dad, husband, and kids (the younger of whom attended only after threats of taking away his electronics) were there. As were two friends from college, their high-school-age kids, and the German exchange student who was spending a full year with them. One of our long-standing holiday traditions is to spend the week between Christmas and New Year playing geeky board games while our kids are left to go quasi-feral. These friends needed to head back to New Jersey that afternoon but decided to hang around to show their bonus German how small-town civics works.

Each swear-ee could choose any book to swear in on and

who would hold it for them. Some went with the good ol' Bible. Because I'm an atheist Unitarian Universalist, which is totally a thing, my husband held a copy of the Constitution. We'd tried to convince the kids to come up to hold it, too, but once they saw there was a newspaper photographer snapping shots, they opted out, lest one of their friends spot them engaging in an activity with their parents.

When I put my right hand on the Constitution and my left in the air, the very nature of the world changed. I clearly saw how all the pieces of government fit together and understood completely my place within that framework. I recited an unbreakable oath to defend all that our nation had stood for for nearly 250 years. The ghosts of Jefferson, Hamilton, and Washington descended into both my heart and mind, and I was at peace.

Just kidding, but, man, wouldn't it have been neat if all that had happened?

In real life, I said some words, promised to do my best for the residents of the county, smiled through the pictures, and sat back down again. Afterward, we ate cookies and steeled ourselves for another trip into the cold.

In our county, any swearing-in ceremony is more for show than to fulfill a legal requirement. That first one on the Hartwick campus was privately arranged for Democratic elected officials. There was a second public swearing in, before the first full county board meeting on January 3. We did it as a group, all fourteen of us with a hand in the air as the county attorney had us repeat the oath of office. Frankly, both ceremonies were lost on me, especially because they had no meaning other than pageantry, and I've never really been a fan of pomp for pomp's sake. I could happily have skipped my high school and college commencements and even my wedding. While I enjoy *having* graduated and *being* married, I've never felt the need to perform them, if that makes sense.

At the start of my life as an elected official, I knew it mattered not one bit on a practical level if I said the oath or raised my hand or spun around in my chair and screamed, "Wheeeeee!" The important part of the induction had happened just before the meeting in the County Clerk's Office, where we all had to sign a white, index-card-size form swearing that we were who we said we were and that we would uphold all the duties of a board member. For me, the creation of a paper trail was the moment when shit got real.

The power of those white pieces of paper became even more apparent when, about eight months into my term, Dan Wilber, the Republican board member who sits next to me and with whom I share my desk snacks, nearly had to step down because he'd failed to sign his white index card before the deadline. Technically—government is big on upholding "technicallys"—he hadn't been a member of the board since January 1. If the board took no action, the county would need to pay for a special election to fill that seat. We'd also need to take a good hard look at all the votes we'd taken since the beginning of the year. Any that wouldn't pass once you subtracted Dan's vote, we'd have to vote on all over again, maybe. Even the county's lawyer wasn't entirely certain what that procedure was, other than unpleasant.

In order to forestall all this, the whole board needed to pass a resolution to say that it was cool that Dan had forgotten to sign the piece of paper but that he needed to do so as soon as the resolution passed. The more strategically minded wondered if there might be a way to get a Democrat in the seat during a special election, but that idea was quashed. I was against it simply because it was a dick move. Others had more reasoned takes.

After we took a few minutes to let Dan know that rules exist, and after Dan apologized for the whole donnybrook, the board voted to let the duly elected (if absentminded) representative stay. Welcome to democracy in action.

◦ ◦ ◦

The main point of the first board meeting of the year is, essentially, to agree to set up a government that will govern through the next calendar year. In theory, all fourteen reps could vote to disband the body and go have lunch. There are days when I regret not having done that.

Forming a government is surprisingly easy when you're using the same one you've had (more or less) since 1791. But before you can do much of anything, the board needs to agree on a chair and a vice chair. On this auspicious day, we held a quiet coup.

For the last couple of years, the board had skewed heavily Republican. One of the driving forces behind getting as many Dems as possible in the 2017 race had been to get the board closer to parity. Having one party control all the levers of government, both on a large scale and small, is less than ideal. I'd say that even if it were my own party in charge. I don't think I'll ever have to say it, given the Democrats' tendency to shoot ourselves in the foot, but I will if it ever comes up. You need a loyal opposition to keep you honest.

For the last few years, Kathy Clark, the Republican representative from the town of Otego—yes, a lot of the place names around here sound very, very similar—was the chair. She'd held on to her seat this year by 12 votes. Kathy is great on an individual human level. I'd trust her with my kids, my dogs, and my last three dollars, even if I can imagine no scenario where I would need to do so. Kathy as the chair, however, was a different story.

The chair sets all the committee assignments, which means she can stack them in her party's favor. She also controls how long debate can last on the floor and how quickly resolutions can be moved. There was a general sense that if you were in Kathy's good graces, you'd be rewarded. If you weren't, well, you were really just occupying space.

In her defense, Kathy had had the hard job of keeping the county solvent during our recent recession. This had meant cutting budgets to the bone when tax revenue dried up because tourism had essentially stopped. It had also meant laying people off, which is never fun. I get that, but that same say-no-first mind-set remains her default even now.

For example, the county business had stalled because it was nearly impossible to pay county employees a decent wage, which meant they were leaving for similar jobs in nearby counties that paid significantly more. Or, worse, they were leaving for private industry and taking their institutional knowledge with them. There was no real motivation for any employee to do his or her best work because all of them knew how desperate the county was to hang on to seasoned employees.

Getting raises into the budget faced resistance at the leadership level, as it would require a significant chunk of change to catch workers up with the prevailing wages. So, the county kept bleeding workers, but the powers-that-be didn't want to pay them more because they kept leaving after a few years and, therefore, weren't worth the investment. You can see where this vicious circle will lead.

This particular can kept getting kicked down the road because the committees and the chair were twitchy about the nation's economic bottom dropping out again. The voices calling for raises weren't calling for large amounts of money, but pointed out that a little bit would save us a whole lot of trouble later. Neither side was inclined to move.

Something needed to break that stasis. That something was the 2017 midterm elections. By the time the dust settled, the board had reached parity, with seven Dems, six Republicans, and one Conservative, who caucused with the Republicans.

Note: The board uses weighted voting, with each seat having a set number of votes to cast based on the population of each district. So, my vote is technically worth just a little bit less than, say, that from the rep for District Nine because fewer people live in my district than his. Rumor has it that this was done to save the county from having to redraw district lines every ten years. Instead, after the census, the number of votes is reapportioned. (I have strong feelings about weighted voting but will spare you the full dissertation on said feelings because it is too nerdy even for me. Short version: Weighted voting does a great job of taking power from the populous areas and giving it to the rural areas. However, resolutions almost never pass or fail because of the way the votes are weighted. It's a quirk of our system that I bring up because if you know it, the official vote counts will make more sense.)

During the weeks between the election and January 1, there had been bipartisan conversations about what the board leadership should look like, given that the voters had decided to balance the power on the board. What if, it was floated, there was a different Republican chair and a new Democratic vice chair? What if, too, the committee heads were also a mix? Over a series of Sundays, we seven Democrats met in a campus classroom to talk this over and to get the four newbies up to speed on what was coming over the horizon.

On the morning of the year's first official board meeting, one of the veteran reps was still counting votes. By the time we started the process of nominating the chair and vice chair, the meeting was starting to feel like a *Survivor* tribal council. It looked like the vote would be in our favor. There could also be unknown alliances at play. The only sure outcome was that

Kathy would be ticked off, regardless of whether she won or lost.

Conflict is not my friend. I blame my being an only child of divorce. When Mom and Dad are fighting, I just want to make peace or hide. Even now, as a grown-ass woman, conflict continues to give me the willies. Yet, I know it is a necessary part of progress.

Before the meeting's start, it looked like Kathy's former vice chair would nominate her for the chair position; instead, he chose to be absent from that day's meeting. When it came time for nominations, only one name was put forward: David Bliss, a Republican from Cooperstown. The vote was tight. We needed half of the total 6,228 weighted votes and got 4,373 for Bliss, with the rest voting no, absent, or abstaining. Once he took the gavel—yes, there is an actual gavel—Democrat Gary Koutnik was nominated and elected as vice chair. A bipartisan mix of incumbents was named committee chairs. Ta-da! We'd officially agreed to set up a government.

CHAPTER 14

Ethics, Legislation, and Fiscal Policy (Or, Confidence Is What You Have Before You Understand the Problem)

My ability to sit through meetings where I understand less than half of what is going on at any given moment should be listed on my résumé under "Special Skills." I chalk this up to a relentless curiosity about how humans build systems to manage an unmanageable world. Besides, someone needs to ask the obvious questions about the parts of the system everyone else needs a remedial class on. If you really want to understand how, say, the Supplemental Nutrition Assistance Program (aka SNAP) works, explain it to someone who understands nothing about it. I am that someone.

Imagine me in my first board meeting, sitting in my green 1970s wheeled chair behind my official municipal desk, which is at the end of the middle row of the board room, in my most uncomfortable grown-up clothes trying to take it all in. Keep that image in your brain for a bit, because I need to skip forward in time to a workshop that I wish I'd attended before my term started.

The New York State Association of Counties, also known as NYSAC—there are going to be buckets of acronyms for the next little bit; this is how government works: figuring out the clever nickname is a crucial part of a program's birth—holds an annual conference in Albany. During its three days, new legislators attend workshops and presentations with titles such as "Climate Opportunity? Save Money and Create Jobs Through Climate Action," "State Budget Review," and "China's Ban on Recycling Imports and What It Means for Your County."

For the past few years, the conference has been held at the Desmond Hotel, which is nearly on one of the runways at the Albany airport. I'd stayed in the Desmond once, after an incredibly delayed flight back from London, where I had gone to a conference on Lois McMaster Bujold, a science fiction writer. When I walked into the lobby after being bounced through way too many time zones, I figured I was having a hallucination.

The Desmond was built in the early 1970s by John Desmond, a Philadelphia native who was a big fan of mid-Atlantic Colonial architecture. Nearly every public space features brick, tasteful florals, and columns. The four-poster beds are modeled after George and Martha Washington's. Mock storefronts surround the bigger gathering spaces, such as the Fort Orange Courtyard, which includes a koi pond. Everything (rooms, banquet halls, the Tavern restaurant) is under one roof, which is a real selling point in January. In short, the Desmond is like the American pavilion at Epcot in hotel form, only the humans aren't in period dress (which, to me, is a missed opportunity).

The conference rooms in the hotel are, however, like those anywhere, with stackable banquet chairs and foldable eight-foot-long tables. The Town Hall Amphitheater is a step beyond, with stadium seating and all the modern technology a presenter's heart could desire. You get there by walking through the Fort Orange Courtyard, which, during the NYSAC conference, was lined with booths for banks, insurance vendors, and law firms. Just past the indoor gazebo, you turn right onto the King Street Walkway. Be sure to hang on to your map because this hotel is one of those places that scrambles all your internal compasses, including those that track cardinal directions and the passage of time.

There was a separate track of programming for rookie electeds in the Town Hall, a fitting location. As the NYSAC president gave her welcome, I took in the people around me. There were maybe fifty or sixty of us there. I was in the next-to-last row—I had a stupid cold and didn't want to bother anyone else with my box of tissues—and got to watch the backs of quite a few bald white heads. But I also saw gray-haired white lady heads and a couple heads of color. Given how white and male our county board is, I didn't expect the crowd to be as diverse as it was. When Stephen Acquario, NYSAC's executive director, asked who was new to even the idea of joining local government, nearly all our hands shot up.

Incidentally, half a dozen of the women in the room knitted throughout the day, and I kicked myself for thinking it wouldn't be cool to bring my own knitting. When I caught up with one of the knitters during a break, I asked her why she'd run for office. She sort of flapped her hands around, as if taking in the whole country, and said, "It's all a mess." Everyone around her nodded. Some of us sighed.

The conference programming changes a little from year to year. In 2018, the focus was on open government/Freedom of Information laws, local laws, and county clerks. My main takeaway was "I know just enough to be a danger and should check with a lawyer before I open my mouth." This is also good advice for life in general. Feel free to put it on a T-shirt.

When it came to the job of county clerk, what I picked up was that I should listen to the clerk and bring him or her treats. The county clerk was likely in government before you arrived and will likely remain there long after you've gone. Indeed, all your institution's memory sits in the person seated in the clerk's posture-crushing desk chair.

Also on tap was a presentation on the major policy issues moving through the state legislature that year, which meant they would soon become the county's problem (and the state would likely allocate no money for these resolutions). Some of the big policies had already arrived, but there were always others out there waiting to make a tight county budget tighter, such as Raise the Age.

Before I was in county government, I was thrilled to see Raise the Age pass. With this legislation, juveniles who tangle with the law won't be sentenced or jailed as adults. I'm still a fan, mind, but with changes ranging from ensuring 24/7 access to a judge even in far-flung areas of the county to no longer allowing juveniles to be housed with adult populations, I can now see why many of our systems struggle to pay for the law's implementation. While the state is offering some funding, it isn't quite filling the gap. The overview I received that day at the conference offered no solutions, and only flagged the law as an upcoming problem.

From the legislative outlook, we shifted over to talk about budgets. This presentation started with a reminder that New York State's fiscal year starts on April 1; most county budgets, however, start on January 1, and most of the time, the state can't pass its budget until May 1. Because of this, counties frequently have to readjust their budgets once the state gets its act together. This right here tells you all you need to know about the relationship between state and county.

The lunch break in the big ballroom featured a presentation by Thomas DiNapoli, the New York State comptroller. If you ever want to see an old-school New York politician in action, spend some time with DiNapoli. He is charming, brusque, and self-deprecating. Watching him work a room is a master class in schmoozing. I was in awe.

Then it was back for a session on ethics with Steven G. Leventhal, Esq. The longer this presenter talked, the more I realized what bothers me most about the current Republican regime. Yes, yes, I find Trump himself distasteful, but it's the grifters around him who really burn my biscuits. The government works only if the public believes that it is working in their interest. Like Tinkerbell's ability to fly, the government can do its thing only if it has buy-in and trust from We the People, and it's in everyone's best interest not to abuse that trust.

The current administration in DC makes it clear that it couldn't give two shits about what's in the public good and is a million times more concerned with funding the president's next gold-plated vacation home. (Its abuse of the public trust is criminal, actually. It's been maddening to see that no one acting as a gatekeeper has seemed troubled. But if more good people ran for local offices, maybe our action could increase the pressure enough to make them care.)

I can tell how frustrated I was during the ethics session by how scrawling my notes from it are. By the end, all I could do was write down quotes and underline them: "Recusal means recusal" and "In a nutshell, there is no tipping in government."

Leventhal's last quote is the one that rolled around in my head during the hour-long drive home: "Confidence," he said, "is what you have before you understand the problem."

CHAPTER 15

The Room Where It Happens

Once the chair and vice chair have been elected, the year's first board of representatives meeting follows the general outline of every subsequent meeting. Before each monthly meeting, the county clerk assembles all the legislation we'll be voting on. She then sends the inches-thick packet of resolutions to us either via email or actual mail.

Each meeting has four parts: The first part is devoted to discussing all your failures as a governing body, followed by learning something new about how shit you didn't realize needed to get done gets done. Then there's a long discussion that could have been avoided if the reps had read their email, and then voting (with occasional arguing). After those four events, we all go home.

So, we start with the airing of grievances, aka the "privilege of the floor." During this, any Otsego County resident is invited to speak about whatever is on his, her, or their mind. The county's representatives do not respond and let the speakers have their say. This can be a challenge, especially when a constituent's version of events doesn't match what the record says happened.

Privilege of the floor (POTF) wouldn't work in a more populous county unless there were firmer rules in place to keep things moving along. Here, it amounts to a succession of shambling and rambling opinions on almost every bit of business the county touches. The shortest privilege of the floor during my tenure was a brisk fifteen minutes. Most are much, much longer. As a concept, I love the POTF, which shows that the county has made it a priority to listen, even if some individual moments work my last nerve.

During the first meeting with the newly elected board, we heard from a constituent who wanted our first priority to be easy online accessibility to the county laws; another wanted us to vote for her raise; two other Otsegoans wanted us to undo a tax foreclosure on a property from years before; and one constituent wanted us to hire an animal cruelty investigator. One of those four wanted us to know she was praying for us, which was nice enough, I guess, but always feels like the Yankee version of the Southern "Bless your heart." On the surface, both are vaguely nice sentiments whose deep meaning is anything but.

The two people who spoke about the foreclosure issue during my first meeting were frequent fliers. Every month, they return to speak about two tax auctions they believe were unfair, even if they were technically legal. The case has been closed for a couple of years, but these constituents' irritation with the county continues, even though half the representatives involved at the time of the auctions in question are no longer on the board and at least one of them is dead. Some months, there is yelling; others, there is crying. One month, before I was on the board, the meeting was moved to a more secure location because a credible threat of violence had been made by one of the aggrieved parties.

The tax situation is one of those long-standing grudges

where fiction eclipses fact and emotion outweighs logic. While it would be nice to find a solution that makes everyone happy and is legal, there doesn't appear to be one.

There are other regulars, including one who usually starts with a quick sentence about something we've done well and quickly follows it with a list of what we've done poorly. This is succeeded by a talking point from the National Rifle Association or Fox News. This constituent is convinced we need more metal detectors in our schools—schools, by the way, have their own board and are not our responsibility. He'd also like more gas pipelines in the region and thinks that environmental regulations are stifling the county's growth.

He's not the only person in Otsego County concerned with the local energy situation; one of the hot-button issues here is anything even tangentially touching natural gas. Remember our earlier conversation about fracking? I'm still against it, by the way, because it seems like a terrible idea unless you have incredibly ethical extractors involved, which is as unlikely as an old, white billionaire marrying a woman his own age. The problem with admitting that fracking is a problem is that there isn't a cheap and reliable energy alternative in our area. The local power grid is insufficient for the county's needs, and some of our largest employers, such as the colleges and hospitals, have "interruptible power," which means that natural gas can be diverted from them when county usage is high. These and other businesses work around losing that power supply by switching over to burning oil during the coldest days of the winter, when residential demand is highest. In this region, by the way, that is a decent number of days.

New York State Electric and Gas (NYSEG), upstate's biggest power supplier, has pretty much zero intention of increasing Otsego County's capabilities. Local environmentalists insist the gap between supply and demand can be filled with renewables such as solar, wind, and geothermal. However, no one agrees on where wind turbines or solar farms should be installed. In one local town, a few members from an antifracking group have taken over the planning board because they oppose a wind farm in their community, despite being pro-wind in general.

Even if we could agree on where to put the turbines or solar panels, those sources aren't robust enough yet to close the gap, much less expand the supply. Maybe they will be all we could hope for in a decade (and we should certainly invest in them), but that doesn't solve today's problem.

And it is a problem. Light industry doesn't want to move here because we can't guarantee they will have continual power. We could make that promise if there was public support for increasing gas supply by adding another compressor station or a pipeline. But the mention of either of those is like uttering the name Candyman. Horrors will be visited upon thee in the form of letters, visits, phone calls, and privilege-of-the-floor speeches, which are every Otsego Countian's right.

The problem is that the need for energy isn't going anywhere. If there is no pipeline (and, for the record, I am anti-pipeline), there needs to be a compressor station and trucks that deliver to it, which carries a degree of risk. Calling those vehicles "bomb trucks," as if there were a burning fuse sticking out of their tailpipes, adds even more emotional charge to an already fraught argument.

Actions have consequences. Community members are ticked off that a fair amount of development in the county has been slowed because of energy requirements. We can't do much about those requirements because every solution that currently exists is unpalatable. The county would have more leverage with NYSEG to improve service if there were more business for NYSEG in the county, which there isn't because outside businesses don't want to move here because of the interruptible power supply.

Currently, there is a task force devoted to finding solutions. My hope is that at least one workable one will be found. There must be a way to make everyone in the conversation just a little bit unhappy in order to get us to a compromise.

Until then, we'll continue to sit behind our fourteen desks in the 1960s-era meeting room, listen during the privilege-of-the-floor speeches, and work to find common ground.

○ ○ ○

Once we as a board have absorbed all that we have done wrong since the beginning of time—as one of the more seasoned representatives puts it, "We have all the responsibility but none of the power"—we launch into the meeting proper. This part can take up to five hours. We don't stop for lunch, unless a training or executive session will be taking place after the official meeting. In which case, we have been known to order pizza—but not on the county's dime, because that would be wrong.

After the January meeting, during which my hanger reached critical levels, I grew smart enough to always pack enough food to get through an entire day. I keep a supply of emergency peanut butter crackers in my official desk, and I eat the lunch I brought from home as the public's business is done. To do otherwise would be to risk coming completely unglued by 2 p.m. and yelling at everyone because my blood sugar has crashed.

The sheer amount of listening and reporting (to say nothing of the voting) that needs to be done means that moving these monthly meetings to after standard working hours would have them ending in the wee hours of the morning—and we all know that one's best decisions are always made at 2 a.m. and that there is no downside to forcing adults with jobs to pull an all-nighter. Also, I'd need to pack my jammies and pillow along with my snacks in order to make it through.

As I mentioned to everyone while running for office, if we had a county manager, some of this reporting and voting would be taken off our plates. Meetings would be shorter, which means they could start after 5 p.m. and end before we all fell asleep. There is movement toward taking on a manager, and conversations are being had, by the way. We're getting there, but nothing moves quickly. Every couple of months, during POTF, we're told how much of a boondoggle a county manager would be and that we're doing a fine job of messing things up on our own. Turns out, it's harder than you think to change how even a small government operates. But that doesn't mean we stop trying.

After POTF ends, special presentations begin, in which outside agencies, county departments, and advocacy groups that've been invited to appear before the board tell us what they are up to. This is when we learn about new initiatives, such as the local electricity co-op, which is stringing fiber optic lines on its own poles to bring broadband to those without it. And this is when the highway department updates the board about its work improving guardrails and clearing dead trees, two projects that no one thinks about until someone stops doing them.

The occasional college intern will give a presentation on how he spent his time working in the bowels of various county buildings. Watching a young adult light up when she launches into a description of the local solid waste master plan or the need for a co-composter bioreactor gives me hope for the future. I've learned a lot from this Instagram generation—for example, how road crews deploy the "coffee mug test" when evaluating how soon a road needs to be resurfaced: If a passenger can hold a cup of coffee while riding in a car down the road and remain dry, you've got a good road. How wet the passenger get tells you how quickly the road should be put in the budget for resurfacing. Fun, right? Now you know it, too.

After we take our deep dive into, say, the size a septic field needs to be for a Hampton Inn (short answer: very big), it's time for the committee reports. There are seven standing committees and two special committees. More about what happens in a committee—perhaps murder is involved—will be discussed later, but for now, just know that each committee has a board member in charge of giving an overview of what happened during the last committee meeting.

These summaries are as detailed as the committee head chooses to make them, but are almost always based on the minutes that the official county scribe took. Some legislators hit only the highlights: "We voted to fund rabies clinics and tick kits." Others go granular, describing every last upgrade on the new snowplow, from the retractable blade to the automated whirligig that flings the salt. (He probably didn't say "whirligig," by the way. My notes on the snowplow presentation are admittedly thin, mostly because I am the Gertrude Stein of snowplows, in that I believe a plow is a plow is a plow.)

Here's what used to make me crazy about this part of the meeting: if all the reps read their committee minutes, which are sent out shortly after each committee meets, there would be no need to reiterate what happened because we would all know already. How hard is it to read your email and retain the information therein? If you can't retain it long enough, take some notes and bring them with you. This is an open-book test.

After all the business of each committee meeting is reviewed, the board is invited to ask questions. Frequently, there are one or two questions, which we could skip to if everyone read the minutes before the meeting and wrote down the parts that didn't make sense to them. Sometimes there will be a clarification from another committee member who didn't think that the chair explained something well enough. Every now and again, there is a question from a member of whichever committee's work is under discussion because that inquiring committee member missed the meeting. Because I am petty, it takes all my willpower not to lay my head on my desk and sigh heavily when this happens.

Usually by this point in the agenda, the only people in the room are the board members, the clerk and her assistant, the county lawyer, a security guard, a reporter or two from the local papers, and a video camera. The rest of the fifteen to twenty other people who turned up at the start of the meeting will have moved on with the rest of their lives. The minutes taken during the committee reports will only say that they happened and won't record the substance of anything discussed.

Eventually, I figured out that the reporters (and the reps who haven't read the minutes) are our audience. (In theory, the audience is also anyone who watches the video, which is recorded and uploaded to the weekly newspaper's website. I suspect the number of viewers for any given recording can easily fit in a Prius, with room left over for a large dog and a Grande cold brew with which to test the roads. Although what happens in the meetings has more impact on an Otsego County resident than the presidential debates, watching the video would be an even better cure for insomnia than C-SPAN. The latter, at least, has a call-in show.)

Most of what is decided by the county government is decided during these committee meetings. This is where cases are made for adding a job or removing one; buying more bulletproof vests for police officers; or increasing transportation options for veterans. And the reports from the committees are the justifications for why, say, a new snowplow or addiction treatment is worth the money, and are the committee heads' opportunity to show why certain decisions are made. You can get all that from the minutes, but the presentations emphasize what might be most important to someone who didn't read the minutes, such as a reporter (or any of your fellow representatives).

What comes next is voting on all the resolutions that have been generated in committee, approved by the admin committee, and pushed to the full board. In order to speed up this part of the process, we use a "consent agenda." (The Consent Agenda would make a great title for a sex-ed course, by the way, or a punk band.) Rather than vote on each resolution individually, which would move this meeting from "Man, my butt hurts" to "I feel like an empty husk of a human" by quitting time, they are voted on in one big batch. Any rep can pull a piece of legislation to discuss it separately, but once those two or three resolutions are pulled and put in their own special pile, everything else in our inches-thick packet is passed by a roll call vote.

I nearly freaked out during my first roll call vote. I was afraid I'd space out before my name came around and the whole room would have to wait until I realized that it was my turn. Deep, deep down, some part of me will always be back in junior high, trying to act like I'm paying way more attention to the world outside my head than I actually am.

One of the quirks of this system is that any one of us could opt to have all the resolutions read out loud by the clerk of the board. Part of me lives in fear that it will be requested; the other part of me wants to request it just to see it happen.

The resolutions that have been put in time-out are next on the docket. Maybe half will be singled out because of a clerical error—perhaps two numerals were accidentally reversed or an important word was omitted. Still, it is vital to fix these sorts of nitpicky mistakes before a resolution is passed. Let's say we're voting to foreclose on and sell at auction a piece of land with a tax ID number that no one notices is actually the tax ID number for the Baseball Hall of Fame. If that legislation were passed, technically someone could buy that land out from under the foundation that currently owned it. Once such legislation is passed, these sorts of human goofs can be undone, but it is a massive pain in the ass. It's much better to catch them before they happen.

The other half of the resolutions might be controversial, and are pulled by a representative because he or she wants to debate their merits further and/or get everyone's vote for them on the record. In theory, a board member's vote on a hotly contested resolution about, say, selling a piece of property or giving county workers raises could later be cited during a heated election season. I've yet to see this happen, but it could.

One resolution was pulled because a committee member had missed a meeting and hadn't read the minutes before the full board meeting. Years ago, back when the county was improving its 911 coverage (which is tricky with all the mountains and the spotty cell network), it bought three pieces of property on which to install cell phone towers. (The hue and cry by nearby residents worried about having to look at said cell towers is an exercise best left to the reader's imagination.)

Once the towers were built, the land that remained was to be put back on the market. Two of these parcels were sold; one wasn't, not because it had a cell tower on it but because it was tricky to get to and ran contiguous with a park. The view from that chunk of land is phenomenal, by the way. I highly recommend it.

Eventually, the parcel was put up for auction by sealed bid. The highest (and only) bidder was the Otsego Land Trust, which was going to add the parcel to the park beside it, making an even bigger green space. The trust's offer was more than fair and would easily have allowed the county to recoup its costs. All that was needed was the board's okay—which wasn't given because the resolution was pulled by a committee member, whose argument was that selling the parcel to this not-for-profit agency would take the property off the tax rolls, not allow further development, and put the kibosh on deer hunting there. No matter how many times it was explained that (a) the parcel already wasn't on the tax rolls because the county owned it, (b) no developers were lining up to snatch it, and (c) well, okay, he had a point about the deer hunting, he wasn't going to vote for it. For complicated reasons involving a number of reps who had to recuse themselves from the vote or were absent, the bid was rejected. Months later, after making sure the Otsego Land Trust still wanted the property and scouring *Robert's Rules* for the correct way to bring this sale back up for a vote, the county finally sold this chunk of land. The rep who was against it remained against it, but we had enough votes to make a lovely park slightly larger. Hooray.

Sometimes legislation is pulled so that a board member can recuse him- or herself because of a personal connection to the issue at hand. For example, when Kathy's husband was running for sheriff, she pulled any legislation involving that department so that she wouldn't have a vote on it. Remember, a government works only if the people it is governing believe that their representatives are voting in the public's best interest, not their own best interest. If legislation came up that involved, say, the state college in the county, I'd have to recuse myself because I have a vested interest in my employer's success.

But just as in legislatures higher up the chain, pulling a resolution is also used as a signal to a set of voters. Frequently in our county, the voters in question are the business-above-all-else crowd. And any proposal involving climate change is the red flag to their bull.

The Climate Smart Communities program was launched by New York State to encourage greener practices among local governments. Two hundred fifty communities, ranging from wee hamlets to entire counties, have adopted the CSC resolution and taken the required pledge, whose ten tenets essentially make up the resolution. See how many seem like a good idea to you:

1. Build a climate-smart community.
2. Inventory emissions, set goals, and plan for climate action.
3. Decrease energy use.
4. Shift to clean, renewable energy.
5. Use climate-smart materials management.
6. Implement climate-smart land use.
7. Enhance community resilience to climate change.
8. Support a green innovation economy.
9. Inform and inspire the public.
10. Engage in an evolving process of climate action.

◦ ◦ ◦

If you'd like to keep a glacier or two unmelted during the next decade, these tenets are a net positive. My objection to them is that they don't go nearly far enough and have no way of being measured. But the statewide Climate Smart Task Force that drafted them was more clever than bold, and the tenets are about as daring as three-quarters of the state can handle.

Another problem: they aren't binding. If Otsego County decides to start strip-mining coal to burn in its fracking drills, nothing bad will happen. (Well, nothing bad in terms of the state cracking down. It would be bad on a number of other levels.) Meanwhile, adoption of these anodyne tenets opens the county up to new streams of grant money that can help us become a leaner, greener place to live.

The CSC resolution has been before the full board twice. The first time, it was pulled then tabled because no one felt they had enough information to work with in terms of penalties and enticements. Two meetings later, we'd figured out what the implications were if the resolution were adopted: more money maybe and less glacier melting.

I heard from a few constituents that they thought it was a great idea to adopt the ten tenets of the pledge. To each I said, "Yes, I agree with you." I've discovered that people find this response unnerving, as if they believe it should be my default to disagree and provoke a confrontation or that I'm lying to make them happy. But just because I think something is great, it doesn't necessarily mean I can get it passed.

And so, the Climate Smart Communities resolution came around again and was pulled again. Kathy, the former board chair, had concerns that enacting the nonbinding resolution would keep new businesses from coming to the area. Her argument, paraphrased: Why would a business pick a place that wants to decrease energy use when it could pick one that let it use energy with reckless abandon?

Danny, one of the newbies and a staunch environmentalist, offered reasoned responses to each of the business-centric objections Kathy and another board member brought up. Minutes passed, and neither party was inclined to back down. Eventually, enough of us broke the impasse by threatening to "call the question"—code for "For the love of all that's holy, can we just vote already?"

The CSC resolution passed 12–2. Otsego County is now a Climate Smart Community. Please engage with us in the evolving process of climate action—or, you know, move here to build a business that expands our tax base and sucks up all our electricity because this designation does absolutely nothing to stop you. Word of warning: our energy supply is limited and would likely stop you from coming here in the first place, but YOLO.

Once we work through all the pulled resolutions and any that snuck in late, the meeting resembles the last five minutes of a college class. Everyone is packing up their notepads, cell phones, and water bottles to make a break for the door as soon as the bell rings. Once we officially vote to leave the room, that month's main gathering is complete, and all that remains of my official duties are the three committee meetings scattered across my calendar.

CHAPTER 16

Committee Work
(Or, What Do You Do with a Corpse?)

Each county in New York State (and, presumably, in states across the country) has its own structure. One of the more progressive places in New York is Tompkins County, home to Ithaca College and Cornell University as well as the Moosewood Restaurant and about a bazillion Edison-bulb-bedecked bars and headshops. When the weather is cooperative, Tompkins County is a two-hour drive due west from my house.

Tompkins County legislator Amanda Champion and I seem to be living parallel lives. She also represents a District Twelve and is a writer and a knitter. She is also married and has two post-puberty kids. And, as with me, the 2016 election was the catalyst for the overtly political phase of her life to begin.

"I was just completing my MFA from Chatham University when Trump got elected," Champion says. "I heard about the Women's March, and within a couple days I had decided to organize one here. Obviously, folks helped me, and it was a big, amazing event. I was approached after that by the man who was in my current seat on the county legislature. He said, 'Well, have you ever considered running for office?'" The Tompkins County District Twelve representative at that time was considering retiring and was looking around for someone to take his place. "I talked with some other county legislatures and was like, 'Wow, is this something really that I could do?' It's a pretty big change from being a writer," Champion says. "I've kind of always been a bit of an activist, but this was a way that I could get right into the middle of it and be at the table."

At first, it looked like Champion would run unopposed, but at the last minute an independent candidate stepped up. Still, Champion had the Democratic and Working Families endorsements.

"It got kind of tense," she says. The independent candidate put on a pretty good campaign. "She was out knocking on doors just as much as I was. I tried to knock on as many doors as I possibly could, and most people, when you talk to them, they're like, 'Oh, yeah. That sounds great. I'll vote for you.' The day before the election, I went around to almost everyone who had said they would vote for me and just left a note on their door and said: 'Tomorrow's the day. Get out there.'"

Once the excitement of the election passed, Champion and four other new elected officials made a plan to learn about every one of Tompkins County's twenty-seven different departments and affiliated organizations. The excitement and teamwork kept them going. Champion remembers the feeling of "Wow. This is all still new and cool."

She had been attending full board meetings for the better part of the year, but things were different after she was sworn in. "I was definitely nervous. I'm not really a public speaker, so I was kind of like, 'All right. I hope I don't have to say anything,'" she says. "The first time sitting at the table, I was excited and kind of like, 'What am I doing here?' I was definitely wondering if I could do it. Can I live up to what these other people have been doing for years, and how am I going to fit in?"

Now, more than eighteen months into her term, she's figured out some of the tricks of the job. Her advice for newly elected officials is that it's okay to pace yourself. "At first, I really just went for it. I treated it like a full-time job. I took on projects, and I signed up for extra committees," she says. "I learned so much, but by the end of the year I was pretty burnt out.

"We have fourteen legislators for a reason. We all do something different, and we have to trust each other. 'Okay, you're an expert in public safety, fine. I don't need to know anything about public safety. I'll do the environmental piece over here.' This year, I've definitely backed off a little bit and not signed up for extra committees or subcommittees or liaison appointments, and I definitely feel like the work is more sustainable now."

After hearing Champion say this, I suddenly felt less guilty about not knowing every last detail about how snowplows work. I'm glad someone does, and I am equally glad it is not me. In addition to soothing my guilt, she magnified a facet of county work that is hard to internalize until you are there.

"Government moves really slowly, so you can't get it all done in the first three months or the first year. It really does take time, and that's okay," she says. "I still have a lot to learn, but after a year, I sort of get what it's all about. It's empowering to be one of the people at the table and able to stand up for what you believe in. Obviously, it's got its challenging parts. The hardest thing for me is being in the public eye, and that's definitely been a big adjustment."

Another life experience we share is being asked questions about the county no matter where we are. I've been stopped more than a few times while out on a run and have had to apologize for sweating all over the person I'm talking to. We've both been asked questions at the grocery store. While neither of us minds being stopped—it's part of the job—it is tricky when you're trying to buy lettuce and simultaneously answer questions about where the wind farm will be.

In my county, the hot-button topics involve green initiatives and hiring a county manager. In Tompkins, the biggest one at the moment is expanding its airport.

"We've all kind of been like, 'This is great,'" Champion says. "We're getting more gates. We're getting jetways. We're also getting a customs facility, because they want to have smaller jets be able to come in from Canada. Currently, there are people in town who feel like this will become an office for ICE to come into the community and start detaining people," she says. "That is not at all our understanding as a legislature, but people are very convinced that this is what's going to happen. I get why they are afraid, but if ICE wants to come into our community—and they have—it doesn't matter if we have a customs facility. They're going to do it regardless."

This plays into the other discovery about county government Champion has made: it can be trumped by the systems around it. Most people don't understand how it all fits together.

"We have a very engaged population of people who are fighting for human rights, and Ithaca is very progressive," she says. "I agree with all of that. On the other hand, they're really pushing for things hard. We are the county government. There's only so much we can do. We're not the state legislature. We're not the White House."

Even with the challenges, Champion doesn't regret running for office. She will likely run again when her term is up in 2022. (Her term is longer than mine because every county sets its own term lengths.) This is not where she expected to be, but she is enjoying where she has ended up.

"I'm a person who is always open to new experiences," she says. "I've tried a lot of different things in my life. One of my concerns before I ran was 'Oh, gosh, can I do this? I'm just a mom and a writer.' I was thinking just the other day that, yeah, anybody could do this, really. You don't have to be a lawyer. You don't have to be a professor. You can be 'just a mom.' I hope other people come to understand that. The whole point of democracy is to have the people represented by another person. That's pretty much it."

Amanda and I are both proof that regular people can figure out the county government system. But before they do, they have to be willing to be completely and utterly lost within it. Once you start to feel the water of what feels like several million departments, each with its own set of acronyms, lapping over your head, do not panic. Instead, find one small piece of information that you can grab on to and expand upon. For me, that was rabies.

The Health and Education Committee meeting was one of the first I attended after my first main board gathering. Health and Education is the big basket of services that don't fit easily anywhere else. The larger departments we oversee are the Board of Health, the Office of the Aging, Community Services (which itself is a catchall for a bunch of agencies mostly having to do with addiction, mental health, and developmental disabilities), and the coroners. It's like the Circle of Life committee.

I spent the first meeting struggling to wrap my head around the pages and spreadsheets that kept appearing before deciding to just let the data wash over me while hoping for gestalt. That sense of how all the parts work together came to me months later, frankly, but one of the sets of data that lodged in my head was about which animals had been tested for rabies during the last few months. Rabies testing is one of the more easy-to-understand, straightforward jobs the Department of Health does, and the department reports on it during every Health and Education Committee meeting.

I know what rabies is. I have pets, whose shots I keep up to date so that no one in the house winds up like Edgar Allan Poe (allegedly). A good friend had to get prophylactic rabies shots because she might have been bitten by a rabid bat. Because of that, I know that I never, ever want to find myself in a similar situation, because the aftereffects of those shots sound truly terrible. It's like the flu, but for six weeks.

When I saw my first rabies report, I understood it completely. In 2018, thirty-nine people were treated for rabies as a precaution. In those twelve months, seventy-nine animals were tested for the virus, mostly bats, raccoons, cats, and skunks, with a couple of cows, deer, and dogs in the mix. Just to keep it interesting, we also tested a bobcat and a camelid. (It is unclear whether this was a llama, alpaca, or camel, all of which are raised around here for their gorgeous fleece.) Of those tested, two raccoons and a skunk were positive. (The test itself is fatal for the animal.)

Once our committee looks at the rabies numbers, we move along to STD treatment and testing, which is another line item in the health department's budget. In 2018, the county treated 119 residents with an STD (the type isn't documented) and tested 4 for HIV (their results aren't documented). An HIV test costs the county seventy-five dollars. The numbers of people needing STD treatment expand in March, May, and November and are low in the single digits for June, July, and August. The leading hunch for this phenomenon is that college students want to take care of their sexual health before leaving for spring break, at commencement, and before the winter holidays. No one has studied this, but the pattern is unmistakeable.

All this is completely understandable by anyone who has heard of rabies or sex. What's also readily absorbed is that the county's health department is responsible for the control of other infectious diseases, such as polio, mumps, and the measles. Thanks to modern science, we have excellent vaccines that ensure that parents don't have to watch a couple of their kids die before they reach the age of ten. If you think I'm exaggerating, take a stroll through an older cemetery. Keep track of the birth and death dates on the headstones. This alone is a good reason not to want to live in nineteenth-century Scotland.

Most counties in the United States are responsible for making these vaccines available for anyone who wants one, regardless of their ability to pay. The goal is to develop a herd immunity so that there will be a firewall between the disease and those who can't get the vaccine because of allergies or age. The Board of Health has a system to distribute and track all this, because it's in the public's interest to protect itself from highly contagious and preventable manners of death.

Your health department supplies flu vaccines, too. You should get one, even if it isn't 100 percent effective for that year's virus. If naked self-interest in not having the flu isn't enough motivation, do it for your community. Or read about the fifty million people worldwide who died during the 1918 Spanish flu pandemic. It could happen again, if not for the work that these agencies do. (FYI: The county boards of health in New York State also stock up on vaccines and postexposure meds for biological terrorism agents such as anthrax. They are also responsible for developing a plan in case of a widespread attack. If you ever want to succumb to a week's worth of existential horror, talk with a health department staffer about all the gruesome viruses, bacteria, and chemicals they are ready to deal with. You pay taxes so that someone else who knows more about this stuff can deal with it for you.)

One of the reasons we can be so blithe about the fragility of the human body is that our government agencies work so hard behind the scenes to protect us. Their goal is to convince people to act in their best interest even when a cohort decides to resist, putting the rest of the community at risk. In March 2019, after 150 confirmed cases of measles, New York's Rockland County declared a state of emergency and a ban on unvaccinated minors in public places. Those who break the ban will be fined. Rockland is a very short train ride from Manhattan, which had 180 cases by that point. It's hard to say how many kids and seniors would die if there were a widespread measles outbreak in New York City—a recent cluster of cases in Brooklyn was quarantined before it spread too far—but county departments of health do their best to make sure we never find out.

The flu, measles, gonorrhea, and rabies are easy to wrap your head around. The lifting gets heavier when you try to explain how the county pays for it all. In meetings, once talk turns to DSRIP (pronounced DISS-rip) funds and NYSACHO (which I think sounds like "nachos" but am always disappointed to learn has nothing to do with food), I lose all sense of what money is moving from where to where and why it needs to go there in the first place. But the end result is that state or federal money is funneled through the county to pay for STD treatments and rabies vaccines. The most comforting parts of these meetings are when we bounce back to a topic I know, such as radon or Lyme disease, and I am on stable ground again.

At their core, nearly all the departments in the Health and Education Committee link up to a human experience. The Office for the Aging handles just what you'd expect: services for senior citizens, including Meals on Wheels and other feeding programs as well as heating assistance. Our county also organizes tai chi classes geared toward keeping our older residents on their feet and able to balance. Following the funding for this office can also make your head spin, but the end results are clear.

End results lead us to the coroners, of course. (Sorry. I cannot resist an allusion.) The coroner is a vestige from our country's British past. His job was to figure out how and when a person died so that he could collect taxes. It was also up to the coroner to distribute any property and livestock that remained once the Crown took its cut. The word *coroner* allegedly comes from "crowner," or agent of the Crown. It's an elected position because it used to involve mostly taxes and real estate, and voters wanted a say in who was making those determinations.

The job hasn't really changed all that much since its medieval origins. As investigative journalist and author Radley Balko explained in a lengthy opinion piece in the *Washington Post* in 2017, "Until the 1990s, coroners in Mississippi had two responsibilities: investigate suspicious deaths, and round up any stray livestock and return it to its rightful owner. A call to a coroner in the middle of the night could have been to investigate a murder, or it could have been to catch some pigs."

Modern coroners do much more than chase livestock. (This will get a little graphic, so if the idea of no-longer-living bodies lying around makes you a little queasy, you might want to skip ahead.) Indeed, their work touches upon public health, the justice system, and infighting, and the more I learn about how we handle our dead, the more fascinated I become.

The public health part is pretty straightforward: Living people don't want to live around a body that is returning to its original organic molecules. This decay fouls water supplies and does not smell like roses. Just in terms of risk avoidance, a corpse needs to be safely disposed of, usually by burial or cremation.

If we remain in the risk realm, living people also want to know how the former person died. Was it disease? If so, was that disease contagious? Was it a random accident? Or was it intentional and arranged by someone else? Was it old age? In short: Why is this body no longer alive, and will that cause potentially affect others?

Generally, in Otsego County, those two practical concerns are a coroner's problem only if the dead person was unattended when he left the mortal realm. This happens more than you might think. An interstate runs through the county, on which single drivers sometimes have fatal accidents late at night; we have nursing homes where not every patient is watched every minute of every hour of every day; and most addicts overdose alone, as do most people who commit suicide. (Attended deaths have their own routines but are outside the Health and Education Committee's concern.)

A coroner is called to the scene of a death by law enforcement or a health care facility such as a nursing home or hospital. His main job is to remove the body, figure out what needs to be done with it, and determine how the person died. While that all sounds simple, it isn't.

The first part, removal, might be the most straightforward. The coroner shows up and officially says, "Dead." He—I've yet to find a female coroner in the history of the county—then makes note of all the particulars of the body, most of which you've seen on TV: lividity, temperature, and rigor mortis. Photographs are taken, and the coroner decides if an autopsy will be required.

The body is then bagged and tagged, as they say, and the coroner transfers it to his vehicle. Bags and tags are a line item in the budget, as is mileage to and from the scene. Once the deceased is loaded for transport, the coroner needs to figure out where it should go. Sometimes that's easy, as when the person died in a nursing home, a place that usually keeps a form listing next of kin. The coroner calls the next of kin, who makes funeral arrangements, and the loved one's body is transported to a funeral home. If the coroner decides there needs to be an autopsy, he calls a medical examiner and delivers the body to wherever the medical examiner would like it. Either way, his work is then done.

Unfortunately, it's almost never that easy.

Imagine a traffic accident with a solo driver. Eventually you'll be able to track down who the victim is from a driver's license, if he has one on him, or the license plate, if the car isn't stolen. Once you know who the deceased is, you have to figure out next of kin—and that next of kin contact needs to take responsibility for the body and its disposal, which some next of kin don't want to do because the decedent is estranged from his family. Imagine all the ways a person who is struggling with homelessness, addiction, and/or mental illness can die alone without ID. Imagine how estranged he likely is from anyone who might care about him, and how hard those people might be to find.

So, what do you do with a corpse no one wants? If you're lucky, you have an arrangement with a local hospital. Ours allows us one drawer in its morgue for longer-term storage. This arrangement may soon vanish, however, as more health care systems consolidate and try to make profits where they can. According to a white paper (a report advocating a particular policy) from NYSAC—remember this one, the New York State Association of Counties?—"a trend has emerged in which hospitals are closing their morgues to coroners and medical examiners, or hospitals are increasing their costs for body storage and autopsy and toxicology services." Some large counties are building autopsy super centers, for lack of a better term, and charging smaller counties that need such services but lack the funds to build their own.

These autopsy centers are more a vague concept than a concrete plan in our part of the state, and the potential loss of storage space is an issue we're trying to plan for. We have a "mobile morgue" that can hold four bodies when our space in a local hospital's morgue is full. (The mobile morgue, by the way, doesn't wander the county like Baba Yaga's house or anything, but it does have a trailer hitch for those times when it's easier to bring it to the unattended deaths than the deaths to it, as in a multivehicle accident.)

I know. It's all gruesome stuff, but it has to be dealt with— and can you imagine how even more gruesome it would be if no one did anything?

So far, we've not been in a situation where the number of bodies exceeded our capacity for storage. Schoharie County, which is immediately to our north, faced that problem in October 2018. A stretch limo carrying a newly married couple plus fifteen of their friends and siblings lost control on a winding rural road, plowed through an intersection, and crashed into a convenience store. All eighteen in the vehicle plus two bystanders were killed. The accident was as horrible as you'd imagine, and is still under investigation.

Schoharie has even fewer people in it than Otsego, which means it is even less prepared to store that many victims than we are. And we are not at all prepared for that. While next of kin was relatively easy to figure out, the investigation and logistics made finding a place to put everyone a priority. It was eventually sorted out, thanks to the largess of a Schenectady hospital, but not before a giant game of "Not it" was played by different localities.

Again, gruesome, I know. I'm right there with you. But, seriously, someone has to attend to such tragedies.

Back to our hypothetical dead body. In the best-case scenario, in which the coroner determines that no autopsy is required, the next of kin has been tracked down, services are arranged, and transport is complete, the coroner's work on stage two is done.

Now that the body has been collected and delivered to where it ought to be, the coroner has to dig into the last question: How did this person die? In terms of long-term public health, this might be the most important question of all. Is what/who killed this person going to kill more people?

Most Americans are under the impression that the determination of "how" is a science, because that is what our popular entertainment tells us. I'm not judging, mind. *NCIS*'s Abby is one of my favorite characters ever. But as with many real-life situations (childbirth, marriage, divorce, college, vampire slaying), fiction makes it seem much more straightforward than it is.

The crucial fact that unlocks how this system works is this: a coroner is not a medical examiner. The latter is a doctor; the former is pretty much anyone who meets the requirements to get on the ballot. In most places, a coroner has to be over the age of eighteen and live in the county. According to a 2009 report by the National Academy of Sciences, 36 percent of Americans live in counties where minimal special training is required to determine how someone died.

Before we go further, let me state for the record that I am not throwing shade on my county's elected coroners. As far as I know, they are all upstanding men who operate ethically and morally. One of them knows how to tell a great story and is always eager to do so. The issue is the coroner system itself, and it is a system that 1,600 U.S. counties use.

◦ ◦ ◦

As our ability to figure out why someone has died has improved, the coroner system has been called upon to do more investigating. But that isn't what most coroners know how to do because the majority comes from the funeral home industry rather than law enforcement. This can cause its own problems.

A coroner who is also a funeral home director can recommend the services of his own business to families struggling to piece together what to do while still in shock about their loved one's death. Hypothetically, if word of this kind of double dealing got out, the voters would decide if they wanted a coroner who failed to mention all the options for handling the deceased. But before you started reading this, did you give any thought to your county's coroner system? Do you even know you had one? I had no idea until I was in the middle of running for office.

During my time on the Health and Education Committee, after two new coroners were elected, two local funeral home owners reported receiving calls from one of the new coroners, a competing funeral home director, asking them to disclose their price list. Said calls were happening while the coroner was with a family whose loved one's death he was officially in charge of. In one case, the coroner wanted to know if the competing funeral home could offer its services for less than he was proposing to the family, essentially making it clear that he planned to undercut their price.

Is this illegal? Probably not. Is it ethically questionable? Yup—which is exactly what we told these concerned funeral home owners when they presented this information to us and asked to have their letters of concern read into the record. We also had to explain that there was absolutely nothing the committee could do about it. Coroners are elected; therefore, it's up to the voters to decide if they approve of their actions. Unless you can find a way to make Otsego Countians care about the issue, it isn't going to change. And until people are willing to go on the record and make their concerns public via newspaper or television news, no one will know the public even has a say in the matter.

If your coroner system is like ours, the coroners are paid

per call, and it isn't a large sum. No one could be in it for the cash. I have two observations about this: First, unless you're retired, your county work couldn't keep a roof over your head, which might make you more inclined to find ways to leverage it. Second, this makes me wonder if Jessica Fletcher's town in *Murder, She Wrote* had a coroner who was trying to make some extra money by creating more work for himself. (If you are a mystery writer, feel free to use this idea for a plot. You're welcome.)

While I'm putting out the idea of coroner-as-killer as a joke, it does point out another flaw in the system: No one checks the coroner's work. If he decides a death is suspicious, the body is sent to a medical examiner. If he decides it isn't, the body is moved on to the family. Most other jobs in the government have supervision, so much so that it can feel impossible to do the work without getting a dozen other people involved. But the coroner calls his own balls and strikes.

Earlier, in the chapter about my NYSAC orientation and the presentation on ethics by Steven Leventhal, I mentioned that government works only if the public believes that it is working in their interest. I know it's gauche to quote yourself to make your own point, but I'm gonna do it anyway. In the coroner system, there is no way to verify that the elected official is representing the people of the county, who are paying to have this aspect of public health responsibly handled, or is representing his own interests. All you have is the coroner's word, which may or may not be reliable.

Take, for instance, Oneida County, where the paperwork for eighteen deaths at the Mohawk Correctional Facility went unfiled by coroner Kevin Barry from July 2008 to September 2010. According to reporting from the Utica *Observer-Dispatch*, Barry finally filed the reports in January 2011. Then, in July 2011, he failed to file six more; then four more in March 2012.

From Elizabeth Cooper's story in the *Observer-Dispatch*: "Barry said there had been a misunderstanding about where the paperwork was supposed to be sent, and that the autopsies and toxicology reports can take as long as six months to process."

Earlier in the news story, Barry mentioned that his working as both the coroner and a funeral director was responsible for the paperwork delays because he simply had so much to do. Maybe that's all it was, or maybe there are conditions at the jail the public knows nothing about because the coroner has full discretion over what is investigated as a crime, and it is in his best interest to stay on law enforcement's good side. Because there is no transparency, the public simply doesn't know.

When a death occurs and a cause isn't obvious, coroners determine what type of autopsy is performed. There are two options: standard or forensic. In Oneida, standard autopsies cost the county between $600 and $800, and a forensic autopsy costs $1,000 to $1,400. If a coroner suspects a crime caused the death, a pathologist with specialized training is paid to do the more expensive autopsy. The numbers that Cooper uncovered tell a story that doesn't match the county district attorney's expectations. County DA Scott McNamara said he would have expected there to have been about 30 autopsies in 2010, given what came through his office. In fact, to McNamara's surprise, the actual numbers were very different. According to Cooper's reporting, of the 430 coroner calls that year, 160 required autopsies. Of those, 126 were given forensic autopsies, which was four times as many as the DA would have anticipated. That additional cost was passed on to the county.

Given the nature of the coroner system, the public simply doesn't know how the coroner's office operates and if their elected official is protecting the public pocketbook or his own. Barry is no longer the Oneida County coroner, by the way. But he wasn't voted out of office. In 2012, the county eighty-sixed its coroner system and switched to using a medical examiner.

None of these issues is new. Since 1857, the American Medical Association has been calling for coroners to be medical professionals appointed by courts. "This method of filling the office will be more successful in securing the selection of one having the special attainments demanded for the faithful and intelligent performance of its duties than that by popular election," wrote A. J. Semmes, chairman of the National Medical Association's committee to the American Medical Association.

This sentiment was echoed by Balko in his *Washington Post* opinion piece more than 150 years later: "Allowing the official in charge of death investigations to be beholden to political forces is a bad idea, for lots of reasons," he wrote. Some of those are what you'd expect. People who have a vested interest in the outcome—like the sheriff or a prosecutor—usually have the political power to influence the coroner.

"While this obviously isn't the norm," Balko wrote, "it isn't unheard of, and it tends to happen most often when the deceased is part of a marginalized community—where the death isn't deemed 'important.'"

Here's the point where a local conversation dovetails with a national one. As Americans struggle to make our country equitable for all the people who live in it, not just the ones with inherited privilege based on skin color, social class, or sexual identity, we have to look at all the systems that perpetuate imbalance.

"For much of the past century," Balko went on, "coroners played a shameful but often unnoticed role in facilitating lynchings, assassinations, and other racial violence. Too often, coroners' juries determined an obvious lynching to be a suicide or natural death. Even in cases in which they did determine a death to be homicide, they made little to no effort to ascertain the identities of the culprits, as they did in other cases."

ThinkProgress's Aviva Shen wrote about New Orleans city coroner Frank Minyard, who was reelected to the office for forty years before his retirement in 2014. According to civil rights lawyers, some of his cases raise eyebrows, like that of Cayne Miceli, who died while restrained in jail. Minyard and his pathologist said Miceli had died of a drug overdose. An independent autopsy found no drugs in her system but did find that she had severe asthma, which killed her when guards strapped her down flat on her back. Or Adolph Archie, who killed a police officer. Archie was taken from the hospital to the station house, then returned to the hospital. "His face had been kicked in, his skull was fractured, and he had severe hemorrhaging throughout his back and in his testicles," Shen wrote. Coroner Minyard decided that Archie had hurt himself by slipping and falling.

While these cases seem suspicious, we really don't know the truth of the situation—and not knowing is a problem. Even if you discount the social justice issues (a stupid move, in my opinion), coroners with the leeway to make the cause of death whatever is most convenient for them throws a giant wrench into our public health statistics.

Remember, in order to track epidemics, whether they be drug overdoses, suicides, or disease, we need to be able to see how many of them there actually are. We can't even begin to think about prevention until we know there is a problem in need of preventing. The Board of Health is poised to spring into action, but it can't do anything if the coroner doesn't report the death accurately. Balko claims that it was poor coroner reporting that helped the nation's opioid epidemic spread so quickly. That's possible, though our data isn't strong enough for us to know.

Despite 150 years of recommendations to shift from a coroner system to a medical examiner system, counties haven't because there is no political pressure to do so. Without looking it up, do you know how your county handles death? Exactly. If voters don't know, it won't change. (There also may not be enough medical examiners to go around, should everyone make the change at the same time. On this, I'm in *Field of Dreams* mode: If there are more opportunities, the workers will come.)

Before I was in office, my immediate response to hearing about coroners was "Ew," a thought always followed by "That sounds tedious and dull." But as I started peeling away at the topic, I realized how a local approach to death feeds into larger questions about whose deaths are worth investigating and what pressures are in play that might shift an elected official's behavior. This one section of the county organizational chart is a microcosm of how badly government can work when we remove all oversight.

∘ ∘ ∘

Further cementing my status as a nontraditional candidate, I keep starting conversations with "Have I told you about coroners?" It's a weird talking point to hang my hat on, but I am who I am. I'm also working to find out how Otsego can follow Oneida's lead and try something new.

CHAPTER 17

Human Services
(Or, Queer Justice, Government Shutdowns,
and Our Kids)

Not every county solves a problem the same way. When you are looking to change your system, the hope is that you can find another system that works better, then simply copy it. In less populated Texas counties, the justice of the peace is in charge of death inquests, along with marrying people and levying fines for various sorts of misbehavior. Oh, and it's an elected position, with just as many requirements as our coroner's office, which is to say, not many at all.

⊙ ⊙ ⊙

Stacy Hackenberg met the minimal requirements when she ran for justice of the peace in 2017: She was over the age of eighteen—her kids are in their late twenties and early thirties—and had lived in her native Texas for more than one year. The third requirement was a breeze, too: She has lived in Williamson County, which sits on top of Austin's Travis County, for more than six months. Plus, Hackenberg and her spouse could afford the thousand-dollar filing fee.

In many ways, though, Hackenberg was a nontraditional candidate for JP in Texas, which is why I tracked her down.

Her hair is bright superhero blue, she has visible tattoos, and she identifies as queer. Over the years, she's held a variety of jobs. Most recently, she did database marketing, but she's worked in retail, on the American Cancer Society phone lines, and for years as a paid Red Cross trainer for their emergency responder course. She's also volunteered as a Girl Scout leader. But none of her jobs has been in the legal field.

Hackenberg started on her political journey in 2016, when she and her daughter went to their county convention. They were the only two people who showed up from her precinct, which automatically made them delegates for the state convention. Then, she says, November happened.

⊙ ⊙ ⊙

"It was a real shock to see somebody like Trump get elected," Hackenberg says.

She started to take being precinct chair seriously and going to the Williamson County Democrat meetings. Then, in 2017, the Texas Legislature tried to pass a bathroom bill. It was very similar to the bill pushed in North Carolina, which basically said you had to use the bathroom corresponding to the sex indicated on your birth certificate.

"Prior to my active political involvement," she says, "I had been a supporter of the LGBTQ community. So, I went and testified against the bill, both the Senate and House versions."

She wasn't alone. So many Texans wanted to testify that the lines were long. "I waited fourteen hours for my turn to give my testimony. Twice. I keep looking around and wondering why are people in Texas and across the country electing these people who are so clearly not representing the majority thought," she says.

As the year went on, Hackenberg was asked to run for the JP office in her partly suburban, partly rural precinct. She was hesitant because she didn't consider herself the ideal candidate, what with the blue hair and tattoos. Plus, she is "not very good at tolerating stupid people."

Long story short—hint: there was a lot of knocking on doors—Hackenberg won by 89 votes against the incumbent, who had been in office since 1982. "Nobody expected me to win," she says. "I didn't expect me to, but I did, and I just jumped in with both feet."

Jumping in with both feet when you are an inexperienced JP means eighty hours of training your first year, then twenty hours every year after. Hackenberg calls it "baby judge school," and she will have completed the first big block of training by the time you read this. By now, she's able to do the full enchilada of JP duties, which include cases about small claims under ten thousand dollars, truancy, credit card debt, addiction, traffic violations, class C misdemeanors such as possession of drug paraphernalia, and possession of alcohol by a minor. Because Williamson County doesn't have a medical examiner, Hackenberg acts like a New York coroner; she does all the death paperwork and decides if further review is needed.

Oh, and, yes, she performs weddings.

There is a method to Texas's madness when it comes to having nonlawyers as justices of the peace. The intention is that the judge handling these smaller infractions be closer to those they are seeing in their courts. They understand where these people have been and how they might have gotten there.

"We had times when my kids were young that we struggled with income and getting all the bills met," Hackenberg says. "I've been where a lot of these people have been. I understand them. Sometimes circumstances just overwhelm you, and you can't meet all your obligations. Yes, they've broken the law, and they need to have a consequence, but that consequence should be appropriate."

Hackenberg thinks it's important to look at the whole person before deciding on a punishment. On the day we were speaking, she'd had a man in her court who had a ticket for fishing without a license, an infraction that the Texas Parks and Wildlife Department takes very seriously. The fine range is twenty-five to two hundred dollars. The paperwork with the case recommended the maximum, but the JP has discretion.

Hackenberg talked to the guy, who said, "'I've never done this before. I just went out with a friend fishing, and I will never ever, ever fish without a license again. It's just not worth it.' But we keep talking," she continues. "He's in the middle of cancer treatment and on a very limited income. I can tell he's got some health issues 'cause he's having trouble focusing."

Hackenberg reduced the ticket to twenty-five dollars and was able to reduce the court costs to twenty-five as well.

"So, fifty dollars and we're done. How is that?" she said to him and gave him the option of a payment plan or community service. They set it up so that he pays ten dollars a month, and the case is closed.

This is why local offices matter. Williamson County residents chose the kind of person they wanted making these decisions, the ones that will have the most impact on someone's day-to-day life. It's not that federal races aren't important; it's that local offices have more control over your services and, sometimes, your life. After all, the president doesn't know who will be there when you call 911.

Hackenberg points out that one of the reasons there are so many Republicans in higher offices is that their county party found candidates for local office and got them elected. Once there, those officials worked their way up.

"That's where [Democrats] need to be placing our focus," she says. "If we really want to take back the country, we have to start where they started and learn from them. We have to get

Democrats in the county positions and municipal positions so that we have a say in what's going on."

Every single newly elected official who bounds into office hopped up on caffeine and ready to get shit done helps. Every single system is connected to every other system in ways you couldn't possibly foresee. Pulling at what one part of a county does always has consequences in another, and usually in the last place you'd anticipate. It's like trying to get a fitted sheet on a mattress. When you start tugging away to fit that fourth corner, one of the other corners pops off. You get that one squared away, give the first misbehaving corner another go, and have to fold and twist the surface you're putting it on into a new, unsustainable shape. Or, more likely, you realize that you're trying to put a double-size sheet on a queen-size bed and have to reckon with your sheet storage system.

○ ○ ○

Welcome to government.

The fitted sheet scenario is obvious to our county's Human Services Committee, which oversees the Department of Social Services (DSS). This branch of the county government is full of programs for kids and for some adults who live in poverty. (Buckle up for an acronym-a-palooza.)

The DSS is the largest department the county has. It is responsible for a ton of (in terms of paperwork) state-mandated programs. These include services such as adoption, foster care, child protection, child support, juvenile justice, Medicaid, Temporary Assistance for Needy Families (TANF), the Supplemental Nutrition Assistance Program (SNAP), the Home Energy Assistance Program (HEAP), and child care subsidies. Roughly 135 county employees work for DSS, which also contracts out to professionals such as clinical psychologists.

Most DSS funding comes from a combination of federal

and state money, with a local share from the county, to make the books balance. Most of the time, the knowledge that other money is supporting these programs is a boon, even though the compliance requirements necessitate their own set of staff. And the burden of those salaries comes out of every level of funding.

That reliable flow of cash can be stopped when the president and Congress can't agree and decide to shut down DC. Yep. When there's a government shutdown, not only are national parks locked up, but so are SNAP benefits. And without SNAP (which used to be known as food stamps), some Americans won't eat. You can live for a month without going to a park. A month without food is much more challenging.

Ninety-nine times out of a hundred, the shutdowns are short enough that the county can coast a bit until everyone at the federal level agrees to get along again. During the thirty-five days of the 2018–19 shutdown, however, there was a very real possibility that if the stalemate wasn't broken by the end of January, the effects of SNAP's frozen funding would be quickly, painfully felt.

Fortunately, that crisis was averted, but only just. Food banks had spent a week stocking up. DSS was working out how to get basics to people with bare pantries and no grocery money. The whole episode was a blunt example of how national decisions can have local consequences. It was also an example of how hard DSS employees work to reduce human suffering, even if they are not its cause.

DSS is a massive operation that keeps vulnerable people safe, fed, and warm, despite routinely having its resources cut at the state and federal levels while simultaneously having more mandates placed on it. Pile those burdens onto the daily tragedies DSS workers see when they interact with people needing their services—to add insult to injury, half of DSS staff work in a building with a leaky roof and damp desks—and it's no wonder this department sees a turnover rate of 14 percent per year, according to the 2016 Otsego County Strategic Prioritization Plan.

That leaky roof is the responsibility of the Public Works Committee, by the way. While they know all about it, their current focus is on the HVAC units on that roof. At this point, those units are more duct tape and spit than original parts; they needed to be replaced last year—which triggers the questions: Do you fix the roof when you are up there for the HVAC work? Is it better to do one before the other? And how the heck are we going to pay for this? Until those decisions can be made, a number of DSS workers will need their umbrellas indoors.

DSS is also intertwined with the county court system because it processes child support payments, custody arrangements, and juvenile indictments. And that means that it works with law enforcement, too, because some people don't do what the courts tell them they have to do. DSS workers drive all over the county for home visits, which means they need vehicles. Those vehicles are under the purview of the Public Works Committee, but DSS is still required to keep track of certain maintenance schedules and mileage.

Remember when I talked about building cell phone towers? Most of the impetus behind that was to make sure every nook and cranny of the county could access 911. An added bonus is that DSS workers need the cell coverage, too. Not only does it keep them safe when they walk into harrowing situations in strangers' homes, but it also lets them file the bulk of the required documentation from wherever they are.

Or, rather, they *could* do that if they had smartphones or tablets. Until 2017, most of the folks out on the road were still using county-issued flip phones.

Let that sink in for a minute.

The problem with issuing smartphones went beyond merely finding the money. Once we allocated the cash to buy twenty smartphones and twenty tablets, their existence had to be justified to members of the community who insisted that the workers would just play Candy Crush on them all day. DSS had to research types of smartphones and cell service plans, which is its own special nightmare. The purchasing department had to make the actual purchase happen. Then, once the phones were bought, a cell phone policy had to be written and approved by both the department and the parent committee. Our IT department, which takes care of all the computers and makes sure we aren't hacked by outside entities (which has happened at least once in the last two years), needed to get the forty devices ready to use, install high-tech locks and security software on them, and, of course, install an app that would keep the users from playing Candy Crush all day. By the time all that was done, a year had gone by, during which DSS employees continued to schlep back to the office to enter all their case data onto a desktop, which took time away from work they could have been doing out in the field if they had a smartphone like your average thirteen-year-old has.

Oh, and the reason they couldn't use their personal smartphones is because the information they handle is protected by privacy laws, and their phones aren't secure. Still, their employer should have been able to get them the tools they needed quickly to do the job we pay them for.

In a private company, you can make everything happen that needs to happen with one email. But governments aren't private companies. We have to give a public accounting of every nickel spent. All these systems interlock to make sure no one can just run off with the cash box. While I understand all that, some of these safeguards create incredible amounts of friction that make it nearly impossible to do something simple.

Nearly every moment of each DSS committee meeting is about all the parts of the system that are either actively falling apart or about to. Of course, the committee doesn't need to be consulted on the parts of the department that are moving along as they should, but the endless litany of what hasn't worked can grind you down, even when you know other DSS work is going well.

⊙ ⊙ ⊙

Former Oneonta mayor Kim Muller and I talked about the threat of burnout and despair when we met on a bench in the square named after her in the spring of 2019. I mentioned to her that after DSS committee meetings, I'm aching for the merest morsel of good news. Muller remembers that feeling from her time on the board.

"I don't even know if we can get our arms around poverty," I said.

"Just look at the stats on free and reduced lunch in this county," Kim said. "It's a really high percentage of kids."

"Their whole family structure is falling apart," I said. "They need more services than we can provide because it's now generations of kids living in poverty without enough help. You keep peeling back layers, and it's like, 'I don't even know how we can possibly fix this.' So, the best we can do is make sure they have lunch."

"I know. It's hard," Kim said. "I say to people, 'Change one life. Don't always go for the whole forest. Try to take little bits of it—and you make a difference.'"

CHAPTER 18

Affordable Housing
(Or, "Not in My Backyard, or Front Yard, or Within Twenty Square Miles, Frankly")

According to nearly every consultant we've paid over the last twenty years, Otsego County has an affordable housing problem. Personally, I would much rather spend our consultant money on, say, cell phones or mumps vaccines, but I'm told that money can't simply be shifted around like that. The county gets grants to pay for consultants, who produce reports that enable us to get more grants to pay for studies. Studies prove the need for more grants. If you are very lucky, all of that will lead to something useful.

My point: Otsego County has an affordable housing problem, and we have survey after survey that says so. I could have provided evidence of that for a fraction of any one survey's cost. When we moved to Oneonta fifteen years ago, it was impossible to find a rental in the city that wasn't for the college student market and, therefore, didn't smell like weed and wasn't full of loud people. That is not, it turns out, an ideal living situation when you have an infant and intend to have at least one more in the near future.

Because it was such a pain in the rear to rent, we bought a house. Our criteria were simple: Is it in our price range, and is it currently unoccupied? Once we got a better sense of what we wanted, we planned to move into a house we actually liked. The other option was to live in a hotel until a rental opened up somewhere, which was highly unlikely to happen before the infant started high school.

The lack of housing was a problem we were able to solve because of our privilege. Sure, money was tight for six months while we paid the mortgages on our house in Knoxville and the one in Oneonta, but we had enough income and family support to make it work. I'm well aware this is not a solution for most.

I am also well aware that *anecdote* and *data* are not synonyms. However, another anecdote: After twenty years of working in Ohio, my dad retired. He grew up in Pittsburgh, which is where most of his family still is, and had zero reasons to stay in the Buckeye State. Money was a limiting factor— retiring to London was out—but ultimately not a huge issue. Returning to Pittsburgh would have been great, but Oneonta had two things the Steel City did not: his grandchildren.

He spent a year planning his move here. The only problem we kept stumbling into was finding a rental apartment. Dad didn't want to buy a house, mostly because he didn't want to deal with everything that owning a house requires, such as mowing the lawn and shoveling the walk. He also didn't want to own a house in this county, because the vast majority were built before the turn of the twentieth century and have all the quirks that older houses develop. And by "quirks," I mean catastrophic failures of vital systems that happen only in the middle of a Sunday night.

Initially, he was looking for a rental within an easy walk of our charming Main Street and its restaurants. An Ithaca-based developer had just renovated the former department store downtown, turning it into condos. Those condos were perfect for an adult who wanted to be near all the action but also have granite countertops. These were so perfect that they'd been snapped up long before Dad thought about moving, as were all this developer's other projects currently in process downtown.

Eventually, Dad's only real requirement for the rental was that it have a garage. My dad cares deeply about his car and is continually horrified by the state mine is in. After a few fruitless months, we gave up on the garage requirement because it proved impossible.

About four weeks out from his move, he committed to an apartment in a town house development that is thirty years old and looks it. Still, the apartment had a roof and heat, and was unoccupied. Once here, he could look for something more appealing—and he found his current place because my next-door neighbor is a local entrepreneur who also likes to buy old houses, spruce them up, and rent them out. He had a three-unit house across the street that lacked one long-term tenant. Wonder of wonders, it also had a garage.

Not only is that the happy story of how my dad came to live within a fifteen-second walk of me, but it also demonstrates the problems in our housing market. Just to provide some actual data, in a 2017 survey paid for by Opportunities for Otsego, a local agency that "promotes healthy living, thriving families, and caring communities," 84 percent of the 267 survey respondents answered "yes" to the statement "Housing is a problem in our area." In 2018, another consultant (Novogradac and Company) concluded, "There is a lack of good quality housing throughout Otsego County where the majority of housing stock likely exhibits poor to fair condition (both renter and owner-occupied). There is ample demand for additional affordable housing throughout all market areas, both with and without subsidy. However, there has been a lack of new construction since the recent recession."

When you view it from an economic development lens, this means that even when we improve our attractiveness to businesses—maybe just some light Botox and a little lipo—we have nowhere for the workers to live. Unless they want to live in a more rural part of the county or an hour's drive from here, in Albany or Binghamton, there are few options. Talking about housing for gainfully employed or retired people is a pretty damn alluring topic. These are the residents a community wants. The talk gets decidedly less appealing when you bring up shelter for those society wants to pretend don't exist.

When it comes to housing people who don't have houses, two county organizations do the bulk of the work: DSS and Community Services. Both have taken the approach of finding ways to make more housing available for needy populations rather than trying to wedge people into an already overstuffed rental market. Housing those who are struggling is one role for a functional society that reduces suffering where it can. For the less-than-bleeding-hearts among us, not having homeless people wandering the streets makes us more attractive to business investment.

◦ ◦ ◦

Eve Bouboulis, the commissioner of Otsego County's Department of Social Services, found a grant opportunity that would pay for the construction of tiny houses, which are very trendy right now in the housing world. The plan is modeled after a project in Syracuse, and similar such communities are working in places like Detroit, Seattle, and Nashville. Once built, the eight tiny homes would be placed near the Meadows Office Building, home to many of the DSS offices the tiny homes' residents will need. It's also where the Sheriff's Office is located. The homes will have surveillance cameras and staff on site to keep an eye on things.

The advantage of the Meadows site is that it is on a couple of acres of land out in the country. Its closest neighbor is the Cooperstown Holstein Corporation, whose cows seem pretty chill about who lives on the other side of the electric fence. There are other neighbors around the site, but not what you could call close.

The tiny home project came about because State Comptroller Tom DiNapoli noticed that Otsego was paying more for homeless housing (about a million dollars) than the four counties that surround it. He told us to bring that number down, which we've been trying to do, but the lack of decent housing stock is making it a challenge.

While the number of homeless people varies during the year, in the first quarter of 2018, 121 adults and 17 children were housed in motels, and 140 adults and 28 children were housed in other locations, including local shelters. The tiny homes are intended to serve single men and should provide shelter for 18 to 24 people per year. If this program works on a small scale, the plan is to build more such homes.

In late 2018, Otsego County planner Erik Scrivener said to the *Daily Star*, our local paper, "The goal is to gain skills and be on a recovery plan. Hopefully this will be successful, and we can open it up in other places."

There are upsides to the tiny home project, not the least of which is getting people who are living rough on the street into their own place near services they need. The houses themselves were built by SUNY students in Delhi, in nearby Delaware County. They had hands-on experience with construction, plus that choice saved our county a few bucks. Site prep has been done by our public works department with equipment we already have. While that work had to be squeezed in around more pressing obligations, it did get done.

Eve lined up additional grants to build a central building

for laundry and computer access. And if the money works out, she's hoping to put in a garden. The goal is to make this an inviting place for short-term stays. Right now, DSS pays for hotel rooms for clients just entering their system. These tiny homes could get us closer to meeting the comptroller's goal, in addition to being decent places to live. Once a person's life is stabilized, he can be moved into longer-term housing as it becomes available.

The downside to the tiny homes project is pretty much what you'd anticipate: there has been an outcry from those who live near the Meadows Building. Some of their concerns are practical, such as the lights around the tiny homes causing everyone's slice of the night sky to be much brighter than it used to be. There is also a concern that being able to see the tiny homes from their back decks across the farmland will kill their property values.

I mean . . . fine. The lighting issue has been addressed, and a view-blocking tree-lined berm has been erected around the site. What was once an open, well-lit place to live is now decidedly less so, but these requests were not unreasonable. However, the concerns felt less about light pollution and sight lines than about homeless people living nearby. That's an issue that no amount of berm building can solve.

The level of distaste doubles, though, when a project houses people who are not only poor but also recovering addicts. That's the challenge faced by another proposed housing project in the city. Right now, the town houses involved are nowhere near as far along as the tiny homes, but the outcry is already ten times as vigorous.

To explain how all the different agencies, some county, some state, interconnect around this project would be nearly impossible without a couple of hours, a Jenga set, and some strong coffee. The short version: Residential Support Services (RSS), an Albany-area nonprofit dedicated to providing "community-based mental health and substance abuse recovery programs and service," has projects all over the state, including several successful ones already in Otsego County. RSS operates a couple of supported housing units for people with mental illness and addiction—the first opened in 1987—and partners with a local business, the Oneonta Bagel Company, to provide work experience for people getting back on their feet.

In October 2018, RSS released its plan to build a sixty-four-unit affordable housing complex in the Sixth Ward neighborhood of Oneonta. Fifty units will be for workforce housing; fourteen will be set aside for people in recovery. The vacant lot is currently zoned for multifamily apartments. The project will be funded by several state agencies, including New York State Homes and Community Renewal and the Empire State Supportive Housing Initiative. Whatever cost remains will be funded by a traditional bank loan. The city and county aren't being asked to contribute beyond usual city services such as road maintenance and sewage. RSS may ask for a PILOT ("payment in lieu of taxes"), which would essentially mean that they wouldn't pay property taxes for a set amount of time. They haven't yet requested this, nor made it clear that they intend to do so.

Per RSS's brief: "The Riverside Apartments will accomplish the goal of providing much-needed affordable housing in the Oneonta area . . . [A] market study shows strong demand for the project, citing a host of critical variables all working in its favor, including: a limited supply of good quality or new affordable housing in the region; competitive rental rates for all unit types compared to the current market; and a significant number of income-qualified households for all units.

Additionally, there are currently no available permanent supportive housing options for individuals with substance abuse disorder anywhere in Otsego County."

Sounds like a win, yes?

Oh, you sweet summer child.

In all honestly, RSS didn't cover itself in glory when it rolled out its plan. Rather than engage the community for a couple of months before unveiling the scope of the project, it dropped it on the Sixth Ward like a bomb two weeks before a city planning commission meeting. A few more opportunities for input might have saved RSS a number of headaches.

As it stands, the objections to the project are about what you'd expect in any smaller town. The United States doesn't know what to do with people in recovery, and it defaults to keeping them out of sight as best it can. Locally, there are specific objections.

First, Sixth Ward residents already feel like they've done enough to help because a homeless shelter is already located there. The common belief among Sixth Warders is that projects are dumped on them because the residents there tend to have lower incomes. That's not necessarily wrong, mind. But it seems like new housing for workers with lower incomes might be a boon to current Sixth Ward residents with lower incomes who want new housing. These units will also be near the fantastic elementary school where my kids went, and they will have bus service to big-box stores such as Walmart, a grocery, and a kick-ass Boys and Girls Club.

Second, Sixth Ward residents also believe that new construction will be an environmental nightmare, one that will increase the burden on sewage and gas systems and the amount of runoff into local streams. They may have a point, but a complete environmental study has yet to be done. At this point, we really don't know. But we do know that new construction is a heck of a lot more energy efficient than the older housing stock currently there.

The third complaint comes from one particular Sixth Ward resident who has been vocal in his opposition to the proposal. "[I]t doesn't fit into the neighborhood," he said to the local weekly paper. And that is where the heart of the matter lies.

Danny Lapin, who was one of my cohort of new county Democrats in 2017, represents the Sixth Ward. In a letter to the weekly paper, he said, "I am all for building more affordable housing in Oneonta that will provide good homes for hard-working families. But don't be fooled, that's not what RSS is planning. The housing they want to build is primarily for folks receiving public assistance of one form or another.

"Of particular concern to me is the units set aside for individuals recovering from drug and alcohol abuse. According to the National Institute on Drug Abuse, 40 to 60 percent of people with substance-abuse problems in rehab eventually relapse, returning to a life dominated by drinking and illegal drug use. That behavior potentially brings additional social problems and crime to our community."

There's a lot to unpack here, so I'll hit the highlights. There are two big assumptions that should jump right out at a careful reader: first, people who receive some form of public assistance are not hard workers; and second, people in recovery are criminals in waiting.

This letter kicked off a lot of debate in the newspaper comments sections and on social media about what kind of people the Sixth Ward wants in its community. One person who weighed in was Julie Dostal, the executive director of LEAF (Leatherstocking Education on Alcoholism/Addictions Foundation), a local volunteer-based nonprofit agency dedicated to supporting those with addiction. Dostal is in recovery herself.

"Those people get to move into those units because they

have engaged in a treatment or recovery provider to qualify for housing," she wrote in response to Lapin's letter. "They have already made a life decision toward getting better. People with addictions and going through recovery live in every neighborhood. What's the difference if they're living in a housing development or in a house next door?"

Her point is an important one. Your neighbors (not only in the Sixth Ward but all over the county) already include people in recovery. The only difference is that RSS has told you that some of them will live in this complex. Apparently, that makes all the difference.

○ ○ ○

One of the retorts that keeps being interjected into the conversation is directed at those who don't live in the Sixth Ward: "Why don't you build it in your neighborhood if you like it so much?" Given that my neighborhood has more than its fair share of houses occupied by college students, many of whom like to barf on my lawn and have no idea that people sleep at 3 a.m., I'd be thrilled to have working families and recovering addicts move in. But that's not the proposal on the table. The Sixth Ward has a space that is perfect for this development. There is a school, and there are stores and transportation. All the plan lacks are supportive neighbors who realize that being working poor or in recovery isn't a crime.

And after that, please do come over to my neighborhood and knock down a couple of the houses owned by absentee landlords who allow them to slowly rot for the tax write-off. That'll free up some space for more affordable apartment units. That's right. Bring it on!

CHAPTER 19

Balancing the People's Budget (Or, You Get the Representation You Pay For)

One of the challenges facing county governments is convincing younger politically motivated people that our work is as important as the work at the state or federal level. Hearing the voices of residents under the age of thirty would be a good start to building a community that works for everyone, rather than just one that works for well-off businesspeople or retirees.

Liz Walters's path to county office was a weird one, even when one considers the twisty road most electeds take. Walters found herself in an at-large Summit County, Ohio, seat in an unusual way.

Her Democratic leanings started when she was a senior in high school. Her grandfather was ill, and her mom was his caregiver. During this time, Walters learned how devastating end-of-life care can be financially, not just for the dying but for those who love them. Within six months, Walters's mom had to declare bankruptcy. "It was an eye-opening moment about the reality of how poor policymaking can be punitive to people who live in the middle," she says. "Those who are a little bit too rich for help, but definitely not rich enough to build wealth or handle emergencies like this."

And what about her twisty path? Right after college, she took a paid internship with the Girl Scouts of the United States of America, in DC, where she lobbied members of Congress on issues that are important to girls, such as STEM education, rural food access, and juvenile justice reform. Most legislators were happy to see her. These issues were easy to support. Plus, she brought Girl Scout Cookies to the meetings. After her postcollege year (and cookie-giving gig) ended, Walters moved back to Ohio for grad school. To pay the bills, she worked the second shift in the same hospice care unit her grandfather had been in. During that time, she saw that many families were all suffering from the same problem: inadequate funding for end-of-life care. Hosting spaghetti dinners or 5K runs to help loved ones die with dignity doesn't raise nearly enough money to do the job.

Right around when this was happening, Walters says, "some guy named Barack Obama" was running for presidential office. She volunteered four days a week for his campaign while finishing up grad school in 2008. Her intention was to work for the IRS when she was done. Instead, she was offered a job with the campaign, which in turn led to connections within Ohio's political circles. Walters went on to work for her hometown congresswoman at home and in DC, and eventually became the executive director for the Ohio Democratic Party. (FYI: she was in her late twenties at the time. Also FYI: I spent most of my late twenties doing more or less nothing.)

In 2015, she decided to run for the Ohio State Senate, mostly because the end of 2014 had been a whirlwind of political crap. The party's gubernatorial candidate was "a disaster," she says. Plus, her mom had gotten sick, and Walters realized it was time for a change. She was eight months into her state senate run when a popular African American politician joined the race. As Walters put it: there were no hard feelings when she bowed out.

This is where it gets weird. Shortly before all this, the city of Akron, in the heart of Summit County, had three mayors over the span of two weeks during the summer of 2015. Mayor number one, Don Plusquellic, left the office he had held since 1987 because a newspaper editor called him a "bastard" and one of the city council members threatened to shoot him. (The nature of the beef gets a little muddy after that. But, in short, the mayor had had enough and peaced out.)

Mayor number two, Gary Moneypenny, who had been handpicked by Plusquellic, was sworn in, then stepped down a week later because he'd had a "too personal" encounter with an employee in his office. That's his description of the events, by the way.

When Moneypenny stepped down, the newly elected president of the city council, Jeff Fusco, became mayor number three. He made it pretty clear that he wanted to go back to his city council gig after the mayoral election in November. This announcement set off a game of musical chairs as other council members leapt into the newly competitive mayor's race. The seat was won by Dan Horrigan, who'd been on the city council and was the Summit County clerk of courts. In the middle of all this, the county's political "boss" approached Walters and suggested that she step out of the state senate race and allow herself to be appointed to the county council.

He rattled off a number of reasons that she should join. "But the most interesting point he made," the thirty-three-year-old Walters says, "and the one that resonated the most, was that at the time I took the appointment, I was the only member of council under the age of sixty."

Walters's experience as the youngest on the council has been interesting in "good and bad ways," she says. "You go in expecting *The West Wing*. What you really get is a combination of *Parks and Recreation* and *Veep*. Even for someone like me, who'd worked in politics directly, there was still a romanticism of once you get into the chambers, everything's really professional and competent. And it's just not the case."

Walters isn't throwing shade on her ten colleagues. Her board, like mine, is full of people from different backgrounds and communities; Akron is a big urban center, but agriculture is the fourth-largest employer.

"They are wonderful people," she says, "but they're retired. For them, this is just a way they serve their community one day a week for two hours. There is another member of council now who is about a year younger than me, and he's African American. We bring a unique perspective. For the most part, our colleagues are almost like our aunts and uncles and grandparents. They call us 'kiddo,' and they give us advice. For the most part, they're very supportive of anything we try to do."

In some ways, it's easier for Walters to put her progressive impulses to work in Summit County because it is reliably blue. Ohio as a whole is not blue, and the state's very red decisions about money crush every county equally. Money allocated at a state level reflects the priorities of the state government, and counties of a different color can have their priorities squashed by the other party.

"Every year for the last eight years, local communities have lost money," Walters says. "We've lost money to charter schools. We've lost money to private for-profit development corporations that have no transparency. Who the hell knows where our tax dollars are going?"

That same frustration Walters experiences in Summit has started to bubble up in local governments across the state, regardless of party. "Republican commissioners and Republican city council people—they're all pissed at the state, too. They just don't speak out about it the way we do," she says.

○ ○ ○

Walters and I spent some time talking about what it is like to be new in local government. Whenever anyone asks how it's going, I tell her, my response is always that it is simultaneously the most fascinating and the most tedious thing I have ever done.

People always ask her, "What is the hot-button issue?" Her answer? "I never knew that 911 dispatch would be the nastiest political meeting I ever sat through. It's both an empirically fascinating subject for how government actually functions, but with the tediousness of managing the personalities and the politics of it. You're like, 'Give me a break. Emergency service is not political.'"

We both wonder if more women in local government might change how everything gets done.

"I don't really understand how it ever happened that women were labeled as the emotional ones, because, in my experience, both in an elected position and in working with male candidates and leaders for a decade, that is not the case," Walters says. "There're a lot of power plays in this work because some dude got his feelings hurt. That's not to say that women are without those flaws, and this is one of the ways in which society genders us. Maybe one silver lining to that is that women have always been taught to play well with others and be nice as women, right? And in this realm, that's actually a good thing. Unlike a lot of our male counterparts, you know our natural inclination is to accommodation, is to compromise, and is to kindness."

Even if running for office isn't what women want to do, Walters suggests they look at what power they have and how they can organize it to support other women running for office.

That could mean giving money, organizing volunteers, making phone calls, or whatever else needs to be done. The system in place right now seems to be working better for men, maybe because men are better able to envision themselves in office.

"I meet a lot of young men in this state particularly, who all think they're gonna be president of the United States someday—like, [they] genuinely believe it," Walters says. "Good for them. Maybe one of them will be."

But running for president isn't the only option. In fact, if you want to champion real progress, look to what is going on in your own community. Walters points out that in Ohio, the city of Columbus passed comprehensive gun reform and is currently battling it out in court to get it enacted. Cuyahoga County, where Cleveland is, has a well-funded green sustainability director, whose job is to make the city a more environmentally conscious operation.

"Those are the kinds of things that really give me hope," Walters says. "This is exactly what was supposed to happen in the American political system. Not only a separation of powers, but a separation of levels of government, where you don't have to rely on all three levels of government functioning perfectly to still make progress."

○ ○ ○

In order to make progress, however, each level of government needs to have a solid plan and a list of priorities. And one of the most visible ways to do this is through the annual budget. In my county, as I've mentioned, the fiscal year is the same as the calendar year. Everything moves on that schedule. The representatives' terms are up on December 31 of the odd years (e.g., 2015, 2017, 2019), and the new terms begin on January 1 of the even years (e.g., 2016, 2018, 2020). Budgets are calculated, argued about, and passed during the last three months of every year. Right around when families are gearing up for Halloween, we're hunkering down with calculators.

Assembling a county budget is not completely dissimilar to making a family budget. You look at income and expenses and then do your best to make the two come out roughly even. If they don't, you either try to grow income (a second job, maybe, or sell your least favorite child) or curtail your expenses (no more five-dollar coffees several times a day, and maybe go yachting only twice a week). Beyond that basic similarity of balancing income and expenses, the two types of budgets diverge quickly.

Working with even a tiny county budget like ours ($105 million, give or take) can skew your ability to handle your own finances, by the way. You become accustomed to looking at the numbers in your own checkbook as if they were nothing more than a rounding error. It can be hard to remember that you are feeding only four people in your house, not all the senior citizens who need meals. You need to worry about only one car's upkeep, not 80 oil changes and 320 tire rotations.

Beyond the magnitude of the numbers, there are parts of a family budget the county doesn't need to worry about. Unlike a person, the county is never going to retire. We don't need to invest in an IRA or a 401(k). In fact, we don't want to grow a nest egg at all. Beyond an emergency reserve or two, nearly everything that comes in will be spent. Unlike your personal accounts, none of what comes in is actually your own money. Believe it or not, nearly everyone involved in the county is highly aware that this money is given to us by taxpayers who trust us to handle it wisely.

Even the most accurate budget is based on a series of guesses. Here's what we think our income will look like next year; here's what we think our expenses will be. You can use all the data from past years that you can dig up and consult every economist in a tricounty area. It's still just a big ol' guess, because no one can see the future with complete accuracy.

We know that money coming in will come from various taxes. There's sales tax on, um, sales, and the bed tax, which isn't on beds but on hotel rooms. We also bring in money through a property tax. Schools take a cut of the property tax income, and each school district has its own board to make decisions about where that money is spent.

Beyond that, there will always be surprises.

Maybe the state, whose fiscal year runs from April through March, tucks some goodies into its budget that will help counties deal with all the mandates the governor has signed, such as raising the age at which juveniles are treated as adults. Perhaps through some quirk of the universe, one of the Kardashians visits Cooperstown, and Instagram influencers descend like so many locusts. Our tax income would be fantastic. (Income increases almost never happen, by the way. But it's fun to dream.)

○ ○ ○

In 2011, the state government passed a property tax cap because a segment of New Yorkers had been griping about how much they pay for schools, roads, and social services. The cap is calculated by either the rate of inflation or by 2 percent, whichever is lower. Most years, it has been near 2 percent. Overriding the cap is possible, but only theoretically. The numbers of votes needed to do so make success unlikely.

The problem with the tax cap is that the state keeps passing along legislation that counties have to comply with without giving us extra money to do so. (These are known as "unfunded mandates.") We can't raise taxes without smashing against the cap, which means that something somewhere else needs to be cut.

Once a budget is in place, what can crash it are unforeseen expenses. A tropical storm dumps several feet of rain on the county and washes out three bridges. Sure, the federal government will step in at some point, but we have no idea when or with how much. Until you know, you have to cover the cost.

In the Department of Social Services, we talk about a trifecta of doom: if three situations exist simultaneously, we will be, in a word, fucked. The details of each of these three potential points of badness would take days to explain and, ultimately, aren't terribly interesting. Just know that at any given time, only one is likely to happen. The county could handle two at the same time, if not comfortably. An alignment of all three is possible, but no one has ever experienced it. So, then the question becomes: Do you tie up a big chunk of your budget for a once-in-a-lifetime trifecta and starve other, much-needed daily programs? Or do you play the odds and hope for the best?

These are the kinds of calls you have to make during budget season.

Hang on to that for a minute.

○ ○ ○

One of the expenses that voters never want to see increase are salaries for county employees.

Sure, in the abstract, yes. We can all agree that each and every American should be paid a living wage with full (and affordable) benefits, including vacation and sick days. But when it comes to seeing that line item in a budget that's funded with tax dollars, the abstract becomes very concrete. That makes all the difference, especially if Joan Q. Taxpayer isn't getting a raise that year.

That money could be better spent on filling another pothole or housing another person in crisis, Ms. Taxpayer argues. If you don't pay people what they are worth or, more accurately, more than what they can get paid for doing exactly the same work in a nearby county, employees will leave. I mentioned this earlier, but here's why it's such a problem.

Once employees leave, you've created new problems for yourself. Assuming these employees have been around for longer than a month or two, they've taken all their institutional memory, experience, and training elsewhere. Now you have to find and retrain someone else, and that finding and training takes time, and during that time, the vacant job isn't being done.

Plus, recruiting qualified candidates is a massive pain in the ass when everyone knows your salaries haven't kept pace with regional averages. Working in the government is different in many ways from working in the private sector, and one of those differences is that anyone who cares to look can find out exactly what the job pays. Not only are we as a county searching for the most qualified employees, but qualified employees can search for the county that pays the most.

Fail to pay people for long enough, and you have an even bigger problem on your hands. Yes, you've saved some money, but now no one who is even moderately okay at the job wants to work for you. Morale sinks, and the departments start to fall apart. There aren't enough people who can do what needs to be done. While you paved a few extra miles of road a few years earlier, the entire highway department is in shambles.

No matter how many times you explain this, the idea of raises is still met with resistance.

Fortunately for the county board, most county employees belong to a union, the Civil Service Employees Association, or CSEA. Every couple of years, we—and by "we," I mean the negotiations committee, which I am not on, for good reason: I am terrible at negotiations—sit down with our team and hash out raises, etc., for the next few years. Everyone in the CSEA is covered by those pay increases. They are baked into the budget and happen once the new contract is signed.

There is a subset of county employees who are categorized as M&C, which stands for "Management and Confidential," but I've never heard anyone say the full name. The eighty-eight M&Cs comprise department heads, public defenders, the district attorney, auditors, the sheriff, and clerks. If you think of the county personnel roster as a résumé, M&C employees fall under "Special Skills." They do the work that isn't easy to fit into the union's rigid hierarchy of jobs. When I was elected, they also hadn't had a salary increase in ten years.

Another of the monthly committee meetings I attend is Performance Review and Goal Setting, better known as PRGS, an acronym that just trips off the tongue. It's essentially the personnel paperwork committee. The first part of the title, the "PR," is done every odd year. Department heads, who are responsible for evaluating all the employees under them, come to the committee for review. The process resembles about what you'd expect if you've ever worked in a place that is even vaguely corporate. Pieces of paper are moved around, mostly, and the next year's measurables are set.

My first year on the board was a goal-setting, or GS, year. Now that the balance of power on the board had shifted in some meaningful ways, the big goal we set was to determine how much our M&C staff was underpaid and find a way to pay them more. Oh, and maybe teach them how to set SMART goals, the buzziest of goals that are all the rage in private industry, so that we can do merit raises during the next cycle. (Business speak makes my skin itch, so other members of the committee did the heavy lifting on this necessary project. If SMART goals are what the majority wants, so be it. Clearly, they must work somewhat, otherwise they would have died a

Specific, Measurable, Attainable, Relevant, and Timely death by now.)

Behind the scenes, our personnel director, Penny, and her kick-ass interns assemble a salary study that forms the spine of our justification for paying people the market rate for their labor. Conducting a salary study is something you pay someone to do, but after collecting quotes from a couple of consulting firms, we discovered that we'd rather spend that jaw-dropping amount of money on actual raises than on the study itself. Plus, almost anyone with a couple of working fingers, an okay brain, and a computer can assemble a database.

After hunting down data from sixteen similar counties in the state—we didn't compare ourselves to the counties around New York City, for example, because their cost of living is much higher than ours—Penny had a series of lovely graphs and charts made to show just how underpaid our employees were. Armed with actual information, the committee was then able to make its case to the other representatives during budget talks.

I'd like to say that there was a big, dramatic scene during which someone yelled, "I want the truth!" and I got to yell back, "You can't *handle* the truth!" But there wasn't. The knowledge that M&C folks in Otsego County made a lot less than they could have twenty miles away wasn't a huge revelation. What made the difference were the graphs, because those graphs could also be shown to constituents, who were also then able to understand the need for raises.

All told, it took $500,000 in salary increases just to hit the market standard for our M&C employees. That cool half-mil merely closed the gap. Now we have to figure out how to keep the momentum going, and do crazy stuff like merit raises and yearly cost-of-living increases. It's heartening that the push-back on that expense was minimal. Instead, the pushback was on the raises we voted for ourselves, which, to be honest, makes sense.

There is no great protocol for giving yourself a raise. It's nearly impossible in private industry. Unless you own the company, any compensation is figured out by someone above you. If you are in a union, the union sets the scale. Ditto working for the state in a nonunion gig. You know the scale, and your supervisor decides if you meet the minimum level of competency to keep climbing it.

We work for the people, and in a perfect world, the voters would directly cast a yes or no vote on our wages. But I want you to look deep into your heart and tell me if you can envision giving a raise to anyone who currently represents you. Can you separate emotion from logic? You can see the problem, right? Before I was in this position, even with a politician I liked, I wouldn't have parted with one more dime than I absolutely had to.

In the world in which we live (rather than the perfect one where each day starts with gentle puppy kisses), the voters do have a say in their representatives' compensation. It's an indirect one: vote them out of office if you don't think they've earned their keep. Any raise will be in the next year's budget for all to see. While there are ways to be sneaky about it, such as not mentioning it to anyone and hoping no one notices, we made it clear from the start that the raises were in there. Public grumbling ensued, including from one constituent who spoke his piece during the privilege of the floor. If memory serves, we were asked if we had no decency. A totally fair question, mind, and he was well within his rights to say whatever he wanted. As are you. We draw the line at swearing, however, so plan accordingly.

The problem with asking us a question during POTF is that we can't answer. The deal is that you get to say whatever you need to say, and we listen. If you want an answer, ask one of us directly at any other time than during POTF. Each of us will do our best to tell you what we know.

One of the gentlemen involved in the long-standing tax dispute, who has spoken at every meeting for at least two years, commiserated with the "have you no decency" guy, who was angry that we didn't respond. "They never do," he said. To which I wanted to say, "*Exactly.*"

But if I could have said something about giving ourselves raises, I would have said this:

I don't like it, either. I wish there were another way, on this and on so many other hard choices we have to make. If you come up with a real solution, we'd all be thrilled to hear it. Until that happens, this is why we're doing it this way.

And lest you think Otsego County representatives are buying fancy coffees every weekday and two on Sunday, know that before the raise, we each made $10,500 annually. There are also benefits, such as health insurance, which I didn't sign up for because the state benefits through my husband's plan are better.

For me, the take-home pay is roughly $740 per month. I knew this when I ran. Again, for me, it didn't matter one way or another, because county work isn't my sole source of income. After a couple of months on the board, I chose to go part time at my actual job because I could no longer predict how long I would be out of the office for any given county meeting. Most of the time, committee meetings run for two hours, unless they run for four. Full board meetings run for four hours, unless they run for six. The problem with working full time is that your boss actually expects you to be there when you say you will. Crazy, I know.

I am in a sweet spot where I can combine my part-time pay with my county ducats and some freelance gigs, and survive.

I could not do this if (a) I wasn't married or (b) my husband didn't have a better-paying job. Basically, there's a reason that local elected officials tend to be independent businesspeople or retired. Their schedules have more give in them and/or they don't have to worry about income. If you have small kids and you need to pay for day care; if you need to work a traditional forty-hour week to survive on one salary; or if you are working shifts at the mall and have no control over when they are, you will never be able to serve in local government.

While I'm fairly certain our county will never pay enough to get a more diverse set of butts in the board seats, we did sweeten the pot as much as we could. As of January 1, 2019, every rep now makes $13,415. I'm not going to lie and say that I sign the extra few hundred bucks back over to the county every month. The extra cash has been nice and helps cover my gas (and snacks) as I drive from meeting to meeting. I knew what I was getting into when I ran for office. I also knew what I was giving up, and I knew that I was in a rarefied position to make the choice to serve. Most of the people whose voices also should be heard still can't make that choice. But maybe this pay raise will inch us a little bit closer.

That's why I voted to give myself a raise: a little self-interest and a lot of hope.

And I don't know that I could have voted for my own raise if the county hadn't had a decent year in terms of income. It's been a great few years for tourism in our county. For example, the Baseball Hall of Fame is expected to break all attendance records if Derek Jeter is in the 2020 class. Our hotels are full enough, and custom at our retail stores is brisk enough to give the county a little cushion.

Ten years ago, the economy was slowly eating itself. County staff was laid off because money had to go to vital services, such as salt for the roads, heat for the buildings, and vaccines for the babies. And bad times will come around again; they always do. But we can't always be in a defensive crouch, because losing great employees now or cutting giant holes in the social safety net now will hurt us now *and* later. The trick is figuring out how to get it all to balance when there is no perfect solution.

CHAPTER 20

My County Rep Bucket List

Now, after eighteen months on the board, I have begun to assemble a County Rep Bucket List. But instead of a list of wonderful experiences I hope to have, this list is full of tedious or outright weird moments that are bound to come my way. So, it's more of a reverse bucket list: I'd prefer *not to do any of the items on it before I leave, though I know I will be forced to anyway.*

It's also not really a list so much as a number of entries that I've jotted into the margins of my notes. Things like "Be called a Nazi during privilege of the floor," "Pray for the sweet release of death during budget season," and "Sit in a meeting that takes longer than my labor for my first child."

A couple of these feared events have happened already. In a recent POTF, my fellow reps were accused of using tactics straight out of Nazi Germany. We were also called tyrants by a different person, regarding an entirely different issue. Another speaker mentioned that one of the reps was smirking while he was speaking, which resulted in a couple of us standing around after the meeting trying to figure out who it was. I've been known to have Resting Smirk Face, so I assume it was me.

I've only jokingly wished for a nice coma during budget season. I have not yet had a meeting last fourteen hours. But one experience I can cross off my list is "Have an experience with a voter that makes you question if the internet was a good idea."

This happened when a constituent emailed to ask for a meeting so that he could run some ideas by me. It's harder to meet one-on-one with a community member if you are representing a big area. For example, Alexandria Ocasio-Cortez isn't going to show up on someone's front stoop just to chat. (Well, she might, actually.) But in local government, it's totally doable.

The constituent and I found a mutually agreeable time and arranged to meet at a local coffee shop, because even though I am filled with optimism about the local political process, there is no freaking way I'm going by myself to a stranger's house. This is how you wind up the body the jogger finds in the woods at the beginning of *CSI*.

On the appointed day, I bounced down to said coffee shop with a notebook and pen, ready to be dazzled with ideas. I was, indeed, dazzled.

"What party are you in?" my retirement-age constituent asked, shortly after I sat down.

"I'm a Democrat." He flinched. "And I also ran on the Working Party line."

I barely got all that out before he described himself as a pro-life independent Trumper conservative who believed we'd all agree with him if we knew the facts. He gets most of his information from YouTube, he said, and from Candace Owens and Turning Point.

Because of YouTube, he explained, he had dire fears about today's college students and the liberal professors who were teaching them. One of his ideas was to bring his Turning Point pamphlets to a meeting of politically active students so he could show them the facts.

"Students are smarter and more together than you've been led to believe," I said. "I've spent a lot of time around eighteen-to-twenty-two-year-olds over the last fifteen years. They do the dumb stuff that all twenty-year-olds do, but not because of what they are learning. They do dumb stuff because they are twenty years old and still figuring out the world."

I mentioned a couple of ways that the constituent could get in touch with the poli-sci department, which would know what clubs were currently active. He mentioned that he'd be good with just going to campus to talk to anyone who wanted to learn the facts. I explained that because the campus is state property, he had as much right as anyone to use the public spaces there. Plenty of outside groups set up in the quad to speak directly to young people. The young people, I stressed, get to speak directly to you, too.

The conversation rambled on from there. We talked about the DC swamp, which we have very different impressions of. He wanted to set up a vigilante (his word) group to take pictures of drivers who speed on his street because the police should spend their time on drug crime instead. When I explained that his solution would cause about nine different types of legal problems, he let me know that our laws protect the wrong things.

"So, who's above you?" he asked. "Whom do you report to?"

"Voters," I said.

"No. Who is your supervisor?"

I used my notebook and pen to explain how all the layers of government work. Start with the city, the county, then state, then federal. I gave him the name of his city rep, both state reps, and three federal reps. "Schumer is your senator," I said. He knew who Chuck Schumer was. Not a fan.

The conversation closed with his research into JFK's assassination and 9/11, both of which were conspiracies caused by the left, maybe, or the "deep state."

We then said our good-byes and went off into our respective Mondays.

My goal isn't to paint myself as a saint, bringing liberal thought to the red-hatted masses. There is absolutely no chance that I shifted his thinking on any of the topics we discussed, nor was I trying to. All I did, once I figured out this conversation was more about fringe-right propaganda than local issues, was listen.

When there was information I could add, such as that on our government's structure, I did. After he mentioned that the government never gets anything done, I mentioned that an efficient government would be a million times more terrifying than what we have. There is supposed to be some sand in the gears, so that we really think through what might happen.

I entered our encounter with the assumption that his intentions were benign. He just wanted to know how to get his message out to the world. Even though I don't agree with said message, it doesn't mean he doesn't get to speak it. As long as the intention remains persuasion rather than brute force or naked hatred, you get to speak. And other people get to disagree.

The whole exchange would have unfolded much differently if we had been in a town hall with a hundred people, each of whom wanted to recruit others to their side. Or if we had been on TV, trying to sell our ideology any way we could by putting on a show for the audience at home. Meeting to speak face-to-face in a coffee shop works, though I'm not sure how you scale it to a county.

There's still no way I'm going alone to his house.

I don't know how this constituent would have responded

to Seema Singh Perez, who in 2017 was elected to represent
Knoxville, Tennessee's Third District. One of the reasons I
wanted to talk with Seema about her experience is that Knoxville is a city I know well. My husband and I lived there for five
years in the late 1990s. He worked in a historic theater downtown and occasionally designed lights for Dollywood shows.
I was the arts and entertainment editor for the weekly paper.
With such a small staff—there were maybe six of us—everyone
read everything, which meant I knew all about the movers and
shakers in town. One of our jokes around the office was that
the city was run by twelve white guys. We even went so far as
to make a list. I believe there was one woman on it.

The city of Knoxville has changed since I lived there during
the mid-nineties through the turn of the millennium. Some
development projects got off the ground and brought life to
some of the more challenged areas. There's a progressive female
mayor now, which I never thought would happen. But reinven-
tion doesn't happen overnight. Two decades isn't long enough
to undo decades of twelve white guys.

As you might have guessed from Seema's name, she's not a
tenth-generation Tennessean. She was born in India, and her
family moved to K-town when she was ten. Her father taught
at the University of Tennessee's College of Social Work. Seema
moved out to Long Island for a few years, then went back home
to be around her family and raise her daughter.

This made me wonder how Seema got herself elected, and
why she wanted to in the first place. When we started talking,
I mentioned that my anger is what drove me into the race for
public office. She felt the same way, and then echoed the title
of this very book you are reading in her answer.

"So many women, I think, have this thing where if someone's got to do it, like if your house needs to be cleaned," she
says, "you just do it. Right now, the house has got to be cleaned.

People say, 'Oh, she wouldn't have won if it hadn't been for Trump and for the timing.' I *wouldn't* have run if it hadn't been for Trump and the timing. Give me credit for that as well."

Like me, Seema leapt into running for office before she thought about it too deeply. "I didn't think this through," she says. "I am actually a very shy, high-anxiety person. As a person of Indian ancestry and a female in the South of the U.S., I've been taught to shut up. I had a courageous thought that I should speak up, but I forgot that that would mean speaking."

○ ○ ○

One of the perks of local government is that the red/blue divide isn't as apparent as it can be on a bigger stage. Both for Seema and me, on 98 percent of the issues that come up, everyone agrees. As Seema says, "How blue or red can garbage pickup be?" Like, do you think the streets shouldn't be filled with trash? It's that last 2 percent of issues that can lead to heated discussions.

"I'm having to just push myself," she says. "I'm usually the only 'no' vote, so it's usually eight to one. I see my role not as a legislator but as a voice at the table that keeps bringing up that there're other people that have other experiences. I'm speaking for the people that never get represented and will never be present there because they're working seven jobs and don't have a car."

Knoxville's city council has an interesting election procedure. Each district runs a primary, and only residents of that district can vote in it. The top two primary candidates from each district are on the citywide ballot for everyone to vote on, even though they will represent only one small slice of the city itself. It's a government structure that's not widely seen, but Knoxville likes it. There were four people in Seema's primary: Seema and three guys. She lives in a pretty conservative area northwest of the city center. She came in second in that race, then won the citywide vote.

This might be apocryphal (though, having lived in Knoxville, I see it as about right), but it has been said that this system of electing representatives is built around a festering core of racism. It was to give the illusion that the black people who lived in East Knoxville had control over their representatives by letting them pick the top two, but that the rest of the city would then get to choose which one was more palatable. "But this was a time when it worked against them," Seema says, "because the city was a little bit more open-minded than my district."

As in many other cities, towns, hamlets, and villages across the country, 2017 was a watershed year for political activism in Knoxville. There was a movement to take control of the city council. All kinds of activist groups, such as Black Lives Matter and Stop School Pushout (a movement to bring fair rather than racist discipline to public schools) joined forces. Seema hooked up with them and thirty loosely affiliated people, who helped her knock on doors. Still, she says, "I worked my butt off. I worked harder than I'd ever worked on anything ever in my life."

So far, she feels that she's had some success in bridging the red/blue divide. "I work with a lot of conservatives," she says. "I'm a social worker, so I'm able to hear things I don't like and not react. That has helped me a great deal in crossing the aisle, or at least in having conversations. This being the South, we are nice to each other's face, and that serves me."

"When I worked as a reporter," I say, "I also mastered the art of never reacting—until later, when I'd go, 'Wow. That happened.'"

But it's harder not to react when what is causing conflict is who you are and where you came from. "I think I'm the first immigrant that's not, like, German or Swedish who has been elected to the city council," Seema says. "It throws a lot of people off because my name is not European. They just see a jumble of letters and then don't deal with me. I joke that if my name is in a drawing and someone pulls it out, they'll look around to see if anyone saw them and then sneak it back in because they don't know what to do with it. They don't even know where to begin.

"I find it most interesting when I'm going to a ribbon cutting or something, and they say, 'All the elected officials please gather here for a picture,' and then to me they say, 'No, honey, this is for the elected officials.'

"I'm unexpected. In the circles that know me, people have been kind to my face. The circles that don't know me just don't even know where to begin. They need to figure it out because there's going to be a lot more of me," she says.

All this "go, girl" drive hasn't come without a cost. Seema was a housewife raising a child on Long Island for years. Now she's in Knoxville, on the city council, and in the process of a divorce. "I sort of lost my mind or found my mind, depending on how you want to put it. I did this, and it threw the balance of power off. My daughter is fifteen. I'm being really honest with you—she's very resentful that now I'm not available to her but to the city.

"These are all normal life things, but just at a different rate because of this very unusual thing I chose to do," she says. "I've lost a whole lot. I regret that, but I can't go back."

In four years, when her term is up, Seema isn't sure she'll run again. It's a tough job, she says. On the other hand, she doesn't want to waste all that she's learned or the connections she's made. Still, it's hard to make these compromises continuously in her own life in order to keep making compromises on the public's behalf.

"Right now, what is most difficult is that a lot of the progressive people who supported me getting into office I'm finding are part of the problem," she says. "They are theoretically progressive but not willing to give up anything that they have in order for there to be equality."

"Is that what surprised you the most?" I ask. "For me, the transition between campaigning and then actually being in the job was a shock because they're totally different skill sets."

In meetings, she says, she feels like her fellow city council members are looking around and not seeing that not everyone in the city is having the same experience. Seema didn't think it would be this hard for people to understand other people's points of view.

"Just last week," she says, "Bloomberg News came out with a story about how Knoxville was the third-worst in income equality in this country. That has put a new fire under me. How do we address the inequalities that exist? Like, do we really need to have three St. Patrick's Day parades? Yeah, I know y'all are white, but really, quit celebrating."

CHAPTER 21

I Believe that We Will Win

The 2018 midterm elections crystallized for me where Otsego County has gone wrong with its approach to politics over the past decade.

In my part of the county, the fight to watch was the election for Congress in New York's Nineteenth Congressional District, which is the U.S. House seat that represents Otsego County. After a long primary battle that had, conservatively, nine thousand candidates in it and attracted the attention of *This American Life*, the nationally syndicated radio program from Chicago Public Media, Antonio Delgado won the nomination. Delgado, who is African American and grew up in Schenectady, was up against John Faso, the incumbent, who was swept into office during the Trump election. Faso spent his two years in DC ignoring all the progressive voices back in his district. For example, he didn't hold town halls unless he could vet everyone in the crowd. His game plan was to ignore anyone not in his Republican base.

This was a completely rational strategy, given how red this part of the state is. In the risk-reward calculation, letting constituents ask you questions for which you have no satisfying answers has no upside. Faso's biggest misstep might have been vowing to a woman protesting outside his office that he would protect her health care and then promptly voting to repeal Obamacare. The clip of that exchange had wall-to-wall national television coverage for most of October.

But in spite of Faso's health care gaffe, Delgado had only a wee sliver of a chance to win. NY19 is a Republican stronghold. Oh, and Delgado isn't white. And if you think that doesn't matter anymore now that we have a had a black president, I have a lovely bridge I'd like to sell you. Delgado's opposition made a lot of unseemly noise about his brief career as a rapper and did their best to convince their white base that this black man would eat them. It was as subtle as David Duke's bedsheet and about as charming.

When Election Day dawned, the polls showed the race as a tie. It would really come down to turnout. The local Democrats set up in Kim Muller's dining room—she put out donuts and a pot of chili—and tabulated data all day. It was BYOL, Bring Your Own Laptop. Poll watchers, who would spend a few hours writing down the names of who had come to vote at any given location, popped in every thirty minutes or so to drop off their lists. We'd go through the voter registration spreadsheets and check off who had shown up. Then, in the late afternoon, another wave of volunteers phoned registered Democrats who hadn't done their duty yet and encouraged them to do so.

Frankly, I'm not sure the phone calls did much good. Does it help to hector potential voters who've just changed into their after-work comfy pants? Personally, I don't know that these were folks who were going to get the job done. Still, it's like in all the old movies where someone is sent for boiling water when a woman is in labor. You don't really need to boil water. It just gives you something to do while you wait.

What we could tell from the lists, however, was that the

turnout numbers were big. Indeed, they seemed almost the same, for a nonpresidential election, as they were in November 2016. We didn't have any idea what that meant, especially in Otsego. A Democratic House candidate hadn't won the county in recent memory. The possibility that one would win in 2018 was super slim, but wouldn't it be marvelous if one did?

Once the polls closed at 9 p.m. and all the chili was gone, we still didn't know anything much—and we wouldn't know for a few days, because it was just that close. It looked like Delgado was carried over the line by the counties closer to New York City and would take the district, which was what happened once each county started to certify the votes. We didn't know how close it had been in Otsego until the official numbers were released two weeks later. Of the 21,213 votes, Faso received 10,577 and Delgado 10,636. For those who don't have their phones handy, that is a difference of 59 votes.

In addition to that squeaker of a win, we had real data to back up what we were feeling while tracking data at Kim Muller's dining room table. Turnout was way up for a mid-term election. The last comparable election was in 2014, when 15,915 voters filled in their ballot for the U.S. House race. Again, the 2018 turnout was closer to the 2016 presidential numbers. Two years before, 24,434 voted in the district, many of them for Trump. If (and this is a big freaking if) we can keep the trend going, 2020's turnout should be spectacular.

I stayed up way too late on Election Night 2018 because I couldn't pull myself away from watching the returns come in. After 10 p.m., all the TV talking heads starting referring to the results as disappointing because Democrats hadn't taken the Senate. This wasn't a blue wave, they lamented, while gently chiding those who thought it might be. Once it because clear that NY19 wasn't going to be called for a good long time, I took my dispirited self off to bed.

And because it's what I do, I got up earlyish so that I could go for a short run before I had to be in the office. There's something about the repetitive motion that encourages my brain to sort out everything it's been chewing on. When I got back home, after high-fiving my son, who was walking out the door for school, I knew why the night before had felt like a letdown. It wasn't that the wave had failed to materialize (and it would become increasingly clear that a big one really had crashed onto the House), it was that I had wanted the wave to be a tsunami big enough to wash the last two years away.

I wanted the election to feel like the end of a movie, where the forces of right and good squash the evildoers. I wanted 2018 to close out the hero's journey, where Luke takes out the Death Star. When they make the movie of the last few years, I'm sure that's how it will end. Rather than simply taking the House, which is a pretty big deal, history will be rewritten so that the crumb bums are booted from the Senate, Merrick Garland is seated on the Supreme Court, and Mueller indicts everyone in the White House. Roll credits.

Only, that's not how actual life works. There is no hero coming to save us, which is both the bad news and the good news. As important as national politics can be, one person can't fix it so that we can all disengage again. We have to rebuild from the ground up, one small office at a time. We have to have the hard conversations in coffee shops and realize that we can't change minds that really don't want to be changed. It's exhausting. It's messy. It's frustrating. But we have to do it anyway. Civilization doesn't just happen.

I keep going back to my conversation with Denise from Trailblazers. She calls running for office one of "the greatest experiences of her life because I got to meet people and listen to them."

Ultimately, she lost by 41 votes, a number she still remembers even years later. But that doesn't make the experience any less valuable. "It made me understand that those people in those homes that I visited are the people who are the fabric of every community, and they are so often left voiceless, because they don't have representation," she said. "In so many places across the country, people don't get involved in local politics because we're mostly focused on what happens every four years in a presidential year. For me, this local stuff is what politics is all about. It's giving local people a say in where their tax money's being spent.

"Even when I lost, I still had people calling me saying, 'What do I do when I have this issue?' You feel good being able to help people and having people know that they have an advocate. Everybody focuses on the big stuff, but we have to drill down to the very basic level of what politics is. It's personal connection," she says.

I don't think there is some grand conclusion that will wrap this all up in a neat package with a pretty bow. Besides, I think our obsession with finding the perfect, ribbon-worthy solution to all our problems is part of what got us into this mess. I also think that this mess, should we make it through it with our wits and our rights more or less intact, will prove to be the kick in the pants we needed to get reengaged.

The best metaphor I can come up with is a running one, but I think even nonrunners will relate. Running long distances makes you reexamine your relationship with discomfort. There is a big difference between "discomfort" and "pain." Pain should make you stop and deal with the root cause; otherwise, you'll make it worse. If you don't deal with pain, eventually, you won't be able to run at all. Your first priority is keeping yourself well.

Discomfort is a different beast and an insidious one. When you are gunning for a new distance or a new personal record, your body gets tired and your brain takes over. Every passing ache—and there are passing aches—is a sign that you are dying. When you are too tired to ignore it, the voice that tells you there's no way you can keep this up gets louder. And it tells you that you will never be good enough, that this challenge is beyond your abilities.

When I ran my first and only marathon in New York City, back before this whole county rep whirlwind started, extreme discomfort settled in near mile ten. The race starts in Staten Island, then goes through Brooklyn, Queens, Manhattan, the Bronx, then back to Manhattan. It's not an even split. You are in Brooklyn for the first thirteen miles of the twenty-six. At around mile ten, I was convinced I would be in Brooklyn forever, that I would die there and no one would notice, because the residents of Brooklyn would simply step around my body to buy their artisanal pickles and cold brew coffee.

I started eyeballing every single subway stop I passed. There were plenty. I had a MetroCard in my pocket, along with some pretzels, mints, and a metal tag with lyrics from *Hamilton* engraved on it. "Look Around, Look Around," it read—which always brings up the lyrics that follow: "How lucky we are to be alive right now."

Only, this didn't feel like luck. That upset voice just kept getting louder. You are an overweight, middle-aged late-onset runner who doesn't belong on this course with all these real runners. Look at them bound past you, like goddamn gazelles. You will never be a gazelle. Your right calf muscle aches. You are dying. Go back to the hotel and have some pie.

Here's the important part: I didn't stop moving forward. Running very slowly while crying is still moving forward. So is walking while muttering "fuck, fuck, fuck." Because what always happens is that if you just keep going, the worst discomfort passes. Despite how low I was during that last Brooklyn mile and the transit into Queens, my oldest child and three of my best grown-up friends were waiting at the bottom of the Queensboro Bridge. The sheer joy I felt when I saw them was worth every second of discomfort. So was the medal, when I finished. After the kids, pets, and spouse were safe, I would run back into a burning house to save that medal from the fire.

I'm going to let you in on the secret: even the gazelles in a race have moments when they want to pack it in because it's hard. Barack Obama kept a plaque on his desk that read, "Hard things are hard," which is a fundamental truth of the universe. The trick to getting through nearly all hard things is to just keep moving forward, tiny step by tiny step. Cherish the moments of joy. Push through the discomfort.

For me, running for and sitting in a county seat has been my marathon. Only, I have no idea how long this particular race will be. I mean, eventually I'll die, and I doubt I'll be in government when I do. But I hope I'll still be in politics, which is the simple act of trying to connect a community so that we can live in a predictable, prosperous way. After the last three years, I've learned that's the heart of what we need to do.

Acknowledgments

I never know which valuable tidbits of information I should acknowledge on an acknowledgments page and always fear leaving someone out. Regardless, here are the people without whom I could never have done any of this.

Thanks go to you, dear reader, for reading. Now is the time to bend that moral arc. Run for office. Make phone calls. Register voters. Write postcards. Knock doors. It's hard at first but ultimately worth it.

Had Charlotte Nelson, Krista Jean Anderson, Sara Marcus, Leslie Danks Burke, Denise King, Kim Muller, Carolyn Wolf-Gould, Amanda Champion, Charles Decker, Elaine DiMasi, Stacy Hackenberg, Liz Walters, and Seema Singh Perez not chosen to answer their email and/or pick up their phones, this would have been a very thin book. Without children's book creator Lisa Horstman's quick sketching pen, this book would be short one map and a lot of charm.

The team at Henry Holt—Hannah Campbell, Jenna Dolan, Rick Pracher, Declan Taintor, Maggie Richards, Jessica Wiener, and Jason Liebman—made me look much smarter and more fascinating than I actually am. Assistant editor Ruby Rose Lee is a font of patience. My editor Barbara Jones is a mighty witch among women.

Elizabeth Kaplan has been my agent longer than my son has been alive and, somehow, neither of us looks a day over forty. She has always told me exactly what she thinks. This is a good thing.

Daniel Alexander Jones is an artist and soul friend whose work flows into my life just when I need it most. Lin-Manuel Miranda is an artist who has no idea who I am but whose *Hamilton* propelled me up First Avenue during the New York City Marathon (I mentioned the marathon, yes?) and convinced me that the American experiment is worth the fight.

Speaking of my country's ever-evolving government and legal system, the voters in Otsego County's District 12 took a chance on me. My colleagues and I are doing our best to make this an increasingly vibrant place to live.

Moving even closer to home, by the time you read this, my oldest child will be ready to vote in the 2020 election, which seems impossible, but here we are. While she and her brother don't find anything I do all that interesting, they are supportive nonetheless.

It is impossible to thank my husband enough for being who he is—and he'd likely deflect any attempts to do so. He will always be my lobster.

About the Author

Adrienne Martini is the current representative for District Twelve to the Otsego County Board of Representatives. She's also an award-winning journalist who's written for *Cooking Light* and the *Washington Post*, among other publications, and the author of *Hillbilly Gothic* and *Sweater Quest*. When not wearing her county government hat, she works for SUNY Oneonta in the alumni office. She lives in Oneonta, New York, with her husband, two kids, two cats, and one corgi.